BIBLICAL SECRETS
OF A
SUPERNATURAL LIFE

School of the Supernatural

BRUCE D. ALLEN

© 2019 by Bruce D Allen

Second Edition 2023

All rights reserved solely by the author. The author guarantees all contents are original and do not infringe upon the legal rights of any other person or work. No part of this book may be reproduced in any form without the permission of the author. The views expressed in this book are not necessarily those of the publisher.

All Scripture quotations, unless otherwise indicated, are taken from the Holy Bible, NEW KING JAMES VERSION®. Copyright© 1982 by Thomas Nelson, Inc. Used by permission. All rights reserved.

Scriptures marked (NASB) are taken from the New American Standard Bible®, Copyright © 1960, 1971, 1977, 1995, 2020 by The Lockman Foundation. All rights reserved.

Scriptures marked (KJV) are from the King James Version, public domain.

Printed in the United States of America.

ISBN-13: 978-1-7347189-2-8

ACKNOWLEDGMENTS

For twenty years now I have been on a journey of discovery. It initiated early one morning upon awakening, when the Holy Spirit asked me a simple question, "Can a man be translated by faith?"

Initially I was confused by the question as I did not have any paradigm for such a concept. However, as I began to pray and search the scriptures, I became increasingly challenged and excited by what I was discovering. Now, twenty years later, I am more versed in this concept and still discovering the unimaginable depths of the Word of God on this subject.

What started out as a simple question has now become a mandate and calling from the Lord and the increasing focus of our ministry in this hour. We have taught countless hours and held many Schools of the Supernatural in many nations on this topic – Translation by Faith. The hunger and response have been overwhelming. The testimonies of those who come have been humbling and awe inspiring. Truly the Lord has been confirming His Word with signs following!

This journey would never have come to pass without the encouragement and support of so many. In particular I must thank...

Brother Sadhu Sundar Selvaraj, who has been a great friend, mentor and never-ending source of encouragement.

My wife Reshma, who has never failed to encourage me and stand with me. Her excitement and participation in our Schools are a great inspiration and treasure to me.

Michael Van Vlymen, who also teaches in our Schools and never ceases to bless me with his zeal and passion to see these truths released to the Body of Christ.

I must also thank Theresa Marzalek for her editing and proofing skills! I will never be able to express how thankful I am in this process.

Finally, I must acknowledge and thank the many who are hungry for the reality of the Kingdom of God and the desire to walk in all that the Lord has for His remnant people in this hour! Together we are discovering and tasting of the 'power of the age to come'!

TABLE OF CONTENTS

Foreword 7

Chapter One
Stepping into Our Identity 11

Chapter Two
Passionate for the Lord 59

Chapter Three
Yielding to the Process 75

Chapter Four
The Power of the Sanctified Imagination 109

Chapter Five
The Realm of Expectation 139

Chapter Six
A Life of Worship 153

Chapter Seven
Follow the Forerunners 169

Chapter Eight
The Eyes of Your Understanding Enlightened 183

Chapter Nine
The Revelation of Light 215

Chapter Ten
You Are Light 255

About the Author ... 271

FOREWORD

More than 10 years ago, we were on a spiritual journey to draw closer to God. The Holy Spirit led us to a conference in Spokane, Washington where we first met Bruce. We were excited to meet a person who taught and lived deep and biblically sound spiritual truth. We were so hungry, and Bruce Allen fed us well. Right then, we wanted to bring him back to Canada to teach others. Interestingly, we could not make it work.

Last year, again the Holy Spirit led us back to Bruce. We reconnected with Bruce, and this time we were able to bring him to Canada. This year, together with Bruce and Reshma, we formed Still Waters International Missions Canada and we held our first school here in Coquitlam, British Columbia, Canada. Our mission is to prepare disciples of Jesus Christ with knowledge and ability as taught in the Bible. We are delighted to report that the school was a success.

We had many wonderful testimonies of personal transformations and healing. One man thanked me profusely for organizing this school as he had never learnt these deep truths. Another wrote how she was healed from an inability to focus and concentrate as well as from chronic fatigue or low energy. She was able to focus and understand everything that was taught and had full energy after a full day of sitting in the school. Many who had depression were healed. These are just some of the many positive testimonies we received for the event.

Ponder these eternal words from the Holy Bible:

"My people are destroyed for lack of knowledge." Hosea 4:6, KJV

"And you will know the truth, and the truth will set you free." John 8:32 ESV

"Wherefore by their fruits ye shall know them." Matthew 7:20 KJV

"It is the Spirit who gives life; the flesh profits nothing. The words that I speak to you are spirit, and they are life." John 6:63

"Heaven and earth shall pass away, but my words shall not pass away." Matthew 24:35

"And they went forth, and preached everywhere, the Lord working with them, and confirming the word with signs following. Amen." Mark 16:20

"He said to him the third time, "Simon, son of Jonah, do you love Me?" Peter was grieved because He said to him the third time, "Do you love Me?" And he said to Him, "Lord, You know all things; You know that I love You." Jesus said to him, "Feed My sheep." John 21:17

Say you just finished a meal and your stomach is full. Will you say then that you do not need to eat ever again? Of course not, we all know we will be hungry and need to eat again.

What about spiritual food? It is the same here, we will grow hungry and thirsty again when we lack the fruit of the Spirit.

FOREWORD

"But the fruit of the Spirit is love, joy, peace, long suffering, kindness, goodness, faithfulness, gentleness, self-control. Against such there is no law." Galatians 5:22-23

Like Peter, Bruce loves our Lord Jesus Christ very much, and he has been faithfully feeding His sheep by teaching His words with the Lord working with him, confirming His words with signs following as evidenced by many signs and healings with written and verbal testimonies, which are the fruits of this message.

In this time of the end, we have already witnessed many things foretold by Jesus in Matthew 24:3-12. Jesus began by saying, "Take heed that no man deceives you".

Bruce's personal walk with the Lord has taught him many deep truths that align with Scripture and by practicing them bear fruit. It is vital that we know these truths to give us the necessary knowledge to understand and respond to events as well as the ability to do greater works and live a Supernatural life as intended by our Lord Jesus Christ.

"Truly, truly, I say to you, whoever believes in me will also do the works that I do; and greater works than these will he do, because I am going to the Father." John 14:12

Bruce has an anointing from our Lord to feed us well, giving us spiritual strength and ability to stand and overcome with our spiritual armor and do the greater works which we are all called to in these perilous end times.

Just as he has fed us and many thousands globally, he can feed you well too!

Dr. Keith and Magdelene Kee
Still Waters International Missions Canada

Chapter One

STEPPING INTO OUR IDENTITY

As we begin this journey, let's start by making a declaration together. Declaring the following over your life will establish your feet on a solid rock and nullify any attempts of the enemy to thwart God's plan for your life:

> "From my position in Christ at God's right hand, I declare that I am loosed from the power and influence of the devil. I declare that all deaf, dumb and blind spirits must leave. I loose myself from all doctrinal error and any teaching that would hinder and block my relationship with God. I call for God's light to fill me to overflowing and dispel all darkness. I declare that I am light just like my heavenly Father. I receive everything that the Lord has for me without reservation."

God's special grace is upon you, and you'll marvel at what the Lord does in this hour. This is your portion—something that God in His wisdom chose to give this generation. I encourage you to respect what the Spirit of God is doing. Don't make assumptions based on what you think, but rather take steps of faith based on what He says. His Word is truth from everlasting to everlasting.

Since Rosh Hashanah in 2001, I've received visitations from the Lord that have impacted me greatly and have provoked me to continue onward into the full promise of the Lord for my life and for this generation. For those unfamiliar with Rosh Hashanah, let me explain:

Rosh Hashanah literally means the "beginning or head of the year" and is the Jewish New Year. The biblical name for this holiday is Yom Teruah, literally "day of shouting / blasting." It is the first of the Jewish High Holy Days called Yamim Nora'im or "Days of Awe" specified by Leviticus 23:23-32, which occur in the early autumn months of September or October.

Rosh Hashanah is a two-day celebration, which begins on the first day of Tishrei, the first month of the Jewish civil year but the seventh month of the ecclesiastical year.

At these times of visitation on Rosh Hashanah, the Lord has directed me to record and understand what He was prophetically communicating because it was a message to the Church. I want to emphatically state that I never asked for these experiences, nor are they about me personally. Yet as part of the Church, I too, receive these prophetic messages and take them to heart.

Many times, when the Lord has visited me, He has communicated with me through visions. Most believers don't understand that visions are language. One third of the Bible came through dreams and visions. God communicates through dreams and visions, so we must realize that we're "hearing His voice" through dreams and visions. These avenues of communication with God were never meant to be unusual occurrences for a select few.

Years ago, the Lord spoke to me in a visitation. "My sheep hear My voice," He said. "So, you should expect visions and dreams. That IS the voice of God." Like myself, and millions of others, you can and will experience visions in many different and personally significant ways.

As a result of numerous personal experiences, the Lord has become my best friend. I love ministering this concept to the youth, then seeing them embrace that close, non-religious relationship with the Lord. Talking about just "kicking it" or "hanging out" with Jesus resonates with them. They hate religion but love relationships.

Jesus has been my best friend for a long time and has manifested Himself to me as:

- Healer and Comforter
- Bridegroom and Lover of My Soul
- King of Glory
- My Best Friend
- My High Priest

I've encountered Him in so many ways with different facets of His character being exemplified that I can't enumerate them all.

Rosh Hashanah on October 3-4, 2016, was one of the most unusual encounters I've had to date. I didn't know how to share this until months after the experience, and by then, the Lord had been giving me greater clarity and understanding of what I had witnessed and experienced.

The Visitation of the Lord

Throughout the past 18 years, each time I've had an encounter with the Lord during the festive season of Rosh Hashanah, it has been during a time of focused worship. For me, that attitude seems to attune my senses and my heart upon the Lord and the spiritual dimension.

This encounter in 2016 was no different. I chose to come before the Lord with intent, expectation and worship while in a service in Manila. Over time, it's become second nature for me to mentally shut out the activities of surrounding crowds of worshippers in a service or even when I'm alone at home.

While standing at that service with 10,000 other voices raised to Him in worship and adoration, I heard the still small voice of the Lord. He said, "Come up here."

When the Lord directs you to "Come up here," it's beyond explanation and far exceeds our ability to communicate. The only way I can describe this is that every cell and atom of my body exploded in overwhelming joy, and suddenly I was there with Him!

Immediately, I found myself standing before Jesus in the heavenly realm. Behind Him I saw what looked like a massive building that reminded me of Solomon's temple as described in Scripture. The temple of God is the throne of God, and because we are the temple of the Holy Spirit, the presence of the Lord IS the temple.

Before this place of His majesty was a sea of glass. As I looked at Jesus, it seemed as if we were standing on a slight rise, so the scene behind Him looked like a valley from our perspective. I cannot categorically say this was in fact the case, but it seemed that way to me at the time.

As I looked over Jesus' shoulder, I saw what appeared to be billions of people on a sea of glass before the throne. They stood silently, but with a palpable sense of expectation, as if they were awaiting a proclamation.

Though my attention was wholly upon Jesus, I was able to see and take in everything around us. I can't explain the totality of awareness that's granted in that dimension other than to say I was "plugged" into the whole of this vast place.

Upon His head was a multifaceted, multijeweled crown of glory that reflected His glory in bright, living colors and resonated with life, light, and worship.

He wore a purple robe of a living material unlike anything I've ever seen. His bearing was both regal and captivating. An unmistakable dignity, authority, power, and majesty resonated from within Him. In a word, He was THE King.

Most amazing was seeing light radiate from the wounds in his hands, feet and side! From those wounds, in that light, we found life!

This experience was not a casual encounter where someone says, "I want to show you something." This was a declaration by the Monarch, the King, THE King of Glory who came to proclaim something.

In the natural realm, your flesh has a voice that speaks so loud at times, that if you don't know how to quiet it down, it will drown out the voice of the Spirit. However, in the realm of the Spirit, your flesh is still, so you hear and comprehend with great clarity. Such was the case in this visitation.

Upon His head was a multifaceted, multijeweled crown of glory that reflected His glory in bright, living colors ... An unmistakable dignity, authority, power, and majesty resonated from within Him. In a word, He was THE King.

The only thing I could do, and the only thing anyone could do when coming into His presence like that, is to worship Him. So, I immediately fell on my face. I had no choice and no recourse.

Something in my spirit in this holy moment said, "Lord, everything You have ever blessed me with in my life—every revelation, every experience, all of my life—I lay it at your feet." I recognized, with a supernatural clarity, the futility and frailty of human flesh, human endeavor, and my overwhelming need for Him.

I love the story of Abram who left Ur of the Chaldees because he heard the voice of the Lord (Genesis 12:1). Without hesitation, he immediately obeyed what he heard (Genesis 12:4). Sometime later, God gave Abraham a promise of an heir, his son Isaac (Genesis 18:10).

Abraham's faith would have been an unusual faith because there was no voice of God in his day. Yet, he heard the voice of God and followed Him. Abraham followed this voice, and God gave him a prophetic promise, saying, "I am going to make your children as the sand of the seas and the stars of heaven" (Genesis 22:17).

God can sneak up on you, sometimes without you even realizing it. While Abraham was walking in the desert, he saw only sand by day and stars by night. The biblical principal from Abraham's story is to keep the promise of God in front of your face because that which you focus on, you'll connect with.

Sometimes we take prophetic words and put them on the shelf of our spiritual display case. We say, "Look at all of these wonderful words I have! How many do you have?" We don't understand foundational biblical principles, therefore is it any wonder we don't receive biblical answers? Just as Abraham did, we're to keep the promises of God before our eyes continually. That biblical principle will release the promises of Scripture to you.

33 years after Isaac was born, God said, "I want you to go offer him up as a burnt sacrifice" (Genesis 22:2). Abraham didn't argue with the Lord. Instead, he said, "Okay, Isaac, let's go!"

> So, Abraham rose early in the morning and saddled his donkey and took two of his young men with him and Isaac, his son; and he split the wood for the burnt offering and arose and went to the place of which God had told him. Then, on the third day, Abraham lifted his eyes and saw the place afar off. And Abraham said to his young men, 'Stay here with the donkey; the lad and I will go yonder and worship, and we will come back to you.'
>
> So, Abraham took the wood of the burnt offering and laid it on Isaac, his son; and he took the fire in his hand, and a knife, and the two of them went together. But Isaac spoke to Abraham, his father, and said, 'My father!'
>
> And he said, 'Here I am, my son.'
>
> Then he said, 'Look, the fire and the wood, but where is the lamb for a burnt offering?'
>
> And Abraham said, 'My son, God will provide for Himself the lamb for a burnt offering.' So, the two of them went together.
>
> Then they came to the place of which God had told him. And Abraham built an altar there and placed the wood in order; and he bound Isaac, his son, and laid him on the altar, upon the wood. And Abraham stretched out his hand and took the knife to slay his son.
>
> But the Angel of the Lord called to him from heaven and said, 'Abraham, Abraham!'
>
> So, he said, 'Here I am.'

And He said, 'Do not lay your hand on the lad, or do anything to him; for now, I know that you fear God, since you have not withheld your son, your only son, from Me'" (Genesis 22:3–12).

And so that day, the third day, he built an altar, bound Isaac, and placed him on the altar. Abraham faced a test: *Do you love the God of the promise more than the promise of God?*

God tested Abraham to see if he loved God more than Isaac, who was the fulfillment of God's promise to Abraham and generations to follow. Abraham passed the test and proved his worthiness because he loved God more.

On October 2, 2016, I experienced this at Jesus' feet as that question resonated in me. Do you love Him more than you love every promise and every good thing He's ever given or will give you? That question was a no-brainer for me!

Another significant point about Abraham's experience is that this is the first place we see Jehovah Jireh, the "Provider" in Scripture.

> "Then Abraham lifted his eyes and looked, and there behind him was a ram caught in a thicket by its horns. So, Abraham went and took the ram, and offered it up for a burnt offering instead of his son. And Abraham called the name of the place, The-Lord-Will-Provide; as it is said to this day, 'In the Mount of the Lord it shall be provided' (Genesis 22:13–14).

Provision comes from a surrendered life, not from the misconception many have which says, "I gave this up for or to God, so He has to give me something back." There's a vast difference between provision and manipulation!

In that moment, as I found myself flooded with that realization, the Lord said, "STAND."

I could see billions of people before the throne of God. As a holy hush permeated my surroundings, the atmosphere became pregnant with anticipation and fulfillment simultaneously. I knew that a strategic proclamation from the Father was about to come forth regarding the prophetic stream of time in which we live.

Communication in heaven is not verbal. You can communicate verbally, but it's the lower form of communication and therefore limiting and somewhat ineffective. You know how verbal communication goes:

"I said left."

"No, you said right."

"I said yes."

"No, you said no."

Married people really understand this!

In heaven, communication is different. Scripturally, the best descriptor for heaven's communication is a word of knowledge or an impartation.

My wife, Reshma, is Indo-Fijian. She's East Indian but was born and raised in Fiji. I can tell you about the beautiful sandy beaches in Fiji, the 86-degree temperature of the surf and crystal-clear water. I could continue with further description painting somewhat of a word picture, yet I can't possibly describe it effectively.

However, in the realm of the spirit, if I wanted to communicate the beauty of the beach in Fiji, it would be complete and overwhelming! If heaven were communicating, you'd personally experience every minute detail of Fiji. And unlike verbal communication, there would be no miscommunication whatsoever.

Because of this supernatural "knowing" imparted to me, I knew that the proclamation about to come forth was significant and had eternal ramifications to the Church on earth.

CHARIOTS OF FIRE AND THE ELIJAH GENERATION

Above the temple/throne, I saw hundreds of millions of chariots of fire.

Jude 14 talks about Enoch being the seventh generation from Adam. This is significant! I discuss this in greater detail in my book, *Prophetic Promise of the 7th Day*, but let me offer a short explanation. 2 Peter 3:8 it states, "But, beloved, do not forget this one thing, that with the Lord one day is as a thousand years, and a thousand years as one day."

From the days that Jesus walked the earth until the turn of the 21st century, we've completed approximately 2,000 years. In line with 2 Peter 3:8, that prophetically signifies two days. We're now early in the morning of the third day.

Historically, we can trace back from Jesus 4,000 years to the time of Adam. From Adam until the turn of the century, we've completed 6000 years, or six days. Therefore, we're also early in the morning of the seventh day. We're an Enoch generation, the seventh generation from Adam. We'll enjoy the privilege of walking with God, and like Enoch, "be not" because we'll be caught up to ever be with the Lord.

We're also an Elijah generation. Scripture says that before the return of Jesus, a people will come forth walking in the spirit and power of Elijah. Malachi 4:5 says, "Behold, I will send you Elijah the prophet before the coming of the great and dreadful day of the Lord."

We are this generation! In 2 Kings 2:11, Elijah went home in a chariot of fire! The revelation God was communicating to me in this visitation is significant.

The proclamation God brought forth was that we're moving into the final dispensation where God is going to see every prophetic promise in Scripture fulfilled and every des-tiny He began in people's lives brought to completion. This is because "faithful is He who called who is also going to do it" (1 Thessalonians 5:24). We've transitioned into a day—a season—of completion!

Enoch and the Book of Mysteries

At this time, I found myself again able to stand, so I arose and stood facing Jesus. In utter awe of the experience, I marveled at the sensory overload and tangible effusive love of God that created the atmosphere around me. As I basked in this love, I noticed an individual separate himself from the multitudes. As he started walking toward us on a slight incline, I noticed that he was carrying a huge book similar to vintage family Bibles that often grace coffee tables.

Beyond the veil, you know even as you are known. When I recognized Enoch (by the spirit) I felt overwhelmed, as I've always wanted to meet him. I thought I would have an opportunity to meet him one day when we're all together in heaven, yet here he was! I noticed that although he wasn't very tall, his presence was overpowering. The spirit of revelation and holiness effusively emanated from him and accompanied a sweet fragrance. I remember thinking, *I love encountering and experiencing the things of heaven!*

As he approached, I saw that he was holding the book with both hands, pressing it close to his chest as if it were something precious. This piqued my interest and I became curious about the volume that was so precious to him. I kept thinking, "What is this book that Enoch is holding?"

He came alongside Jesus without saying a word, then extended the book toward me. Surprised, I grasped the book, and asked, "Sir, what is this?"

"This is the Book of Mysteries that the Lord gave me when I walked on this earth," he said. "Now, take and finish it."

I trembled with the power and glory released through his words and the book I now held. Speechless, great fear came upon me, and I became weak.

Handing me his mantle, he motioned for me to put it on. Words are insufficient to describe this experience. Joy, fear, awe, ecstasy, love, or unworthiness cannot express the immediate rush of emotion and reverence that flowed through my consciousness. I was literally undone!

In awe and excitement, I asked, "Would you lay your hands on me and bless me?"

"No," he responded with amusement in his voice. "The Lord has already blessed and commissioned you!"

As I turned to the Lord, He spoke:

"Go and do all I have commanded of you. I have given you insight, and you have received My purposes and desire for your life. Now I will give you understanding. As you have met Enoch this night and have received his book of mysteries, so, too, you shall receive of his mantle that has been prepared for this day. Move forward in faith and do not hold back. Now the hour has come for My glory to be revealed. Trust Me to perform all that I said I would do, for it shall surely come to pass now."

A Visitation on Rosh Hashanah, 2017

Rosh Hashanah, September 21-22, 2017, was a very unusual beginning of the year for me. In this encounter, we were home, and I was in my study praying. A heavy presence of God permeated the room, and great conviction came upon my heart. Rather than stepping through and engaging what I knew He wanted to reveal to me, I sensed a caution in my heart. A Holy Ghost unction said that in this hour we need to prepare our hearts as never before.

I spent a number of hours that first night praying and asking the Holy Spirit to reveal my heart to me so that I might repent of things that I may have not been aware of because it's time for the Church to be pure and holy.

At the end of that prayer time, God revealed that in this season, if you're not circumspect, aware and cautious of what's going on in your heart, you'll be hindered to that extent. We're to be a Church without spot or blemish.

> "That he might present it to himself a glorious church, not having a spot, or a wrinkle, or any such thing, but that it should be holy and without blemish" (Ephesians 5:27, KJV).

As you engage and learn, you must remain aware and guard your heart. As you purpose to protect your heart, immediately deal with any distraction, unclean thing, or condemnation that comes at you. If we don't confront those hindrances, we're in danger of the enemy's snare to lead us astray.

I prayed through that night and shared with my wife, Reshma, that it was a highly unusual Rosh Hashanah encounter. I had spent the whole evening in that place of cleansing and sanctification, knowing that more would follow. By the second night, the grace remained. Up in my study I began to pray again and was suddenly caught away in the spirit.

I found myself walking on a beautiful, white, sandy tropical beach. I recognized this beach as I had been here about 17 years earlier with the Lord when He first started giving me revelations regarding translation by faith.

In my earlier experience, God had shown me a nice home close to the beach, and I knew it was mine. In this secret place, I could be hidden and safe, and I could find rest from the end time ministry in which I was engaged. As I relaxed in this home, Holy Spirit said, "Go to the beach. You have company."

I headed for the door and left the house, then walked a short path to the sandy shores. As I faced to my left, I witnessed someone who suddenly appeared on the shore.

I didn't know the individual or from where he came, but I discerned he was here with the Lord's blessing. The person looked around and said, "Oh, this is where you live."

This person had supernaturally transported to the beach with the intention of visiting me. The Lord said, "In the days to come there will be places of refuge, a haven, and the only way to get there will be by supernatural transportation." I had forgotten about this vision and encounter until this particular Rosh Hashanah.

Now back on that same beach 17 years later, I was alone with Jesus. As we walked along the beach, the water was on my right side and Jesus on my left.. He talked and shared something that I can't recall as I was distracted by what looked like a ball of light in His hand.

As we walked and talked, enjoying each other's company, He casually threw the ball up in the air and then caught it. It distracted me because each time He tossed it into the air, it emanated a "force," a power that vibrated and flashed with intense light and energy.

"Lord," I said. "What is that?"

"That's revelation knowledge," He said.

"What do You mean?" I asked.

He took me back to the time in my life when I had studied technology. In computing, if you use the Internet, they take the information that you wish to share via the Internet and reduce it down to data packets of information that comprise a whole. These packets are streamed through the Internet in bite or packet size bits, and then re-assembled on your computer to again become legible.

When these packets come to your computer, a "digital handshake" or connection takes place, and then the information sent is "unpackaged." All that we see on our screens comes in small packets that are put back together as something we can understand.

"This is like a packet of information," Jesus said, as He continued walking and tossing the ball of light in the air. Finally, He said, "Catch!" and threw the light at me.

He's got quite a pitching arm! It came so fast I was unable to catch the "ball" and it hit me right in the chest and went into me. Though I expected to experience pain, what happened was nothing that I had expected. I felt a surge of revelation as if the light was a living thing within me.

"Lord," I said. "What am I supposed to do with this?"

He simply said, "Unpack it."

"How do I do that?" I asked. "How can that happen?"

"I've invested revelation knowledge in you," He said with a serious expression. "And now, as you spend time in prayer and the

Word, I will unpack that revelation and you will begin to walk in this newness of life."

An Increased Rate of Revelation

Because I knew the visitation I received on Rosh Hashanah was not about me but about what He's releasing to the Church, I asked, "What does it mean for this generation?"

"I'm going to begin to release revelation to this generation at an accelerated rate, because this generation will usher in the return of Messiah," He said. "They will walk in the powers of the age to come, but they must receive it by faith."

"Okay," I replied as we kept walking. Suddenly, I looked on my left out to sea where dark massive clouds appeared on the horizon. A powerful storm was coming, and it was moving fast! Nervousness crept in as we continued walking away from the safety of the house; the growing distance made me wonder if we'd be able to return before the storm struck.

I glanced at the brewing storm intermittently. "Don't worry about that as it can't come here," Jesus said. "In this place, you are protected. My people will be granted access to a realm that is untouched by the natural realm. To get here, they must unlock the revelation of who they truly are."

These two visitations at Rosh Hashanah are merely two examples of what the Lord is saying and releasing in this hour. I could (and will) recount many instances of visitation and translation that could fill another volume. My purpose in sharing these experiences is to instruct and provoke the reader to a greater hunger for Him.

I'm not someone special because I frequently experience encounters like this. I'm just like you, passionately hungry for more of Jesus. This is how He's responding to that cry in this dispensation.

The Destiny of God

We're in a season of profound fulfillment of the promises of God for our lives and our generation. Some who read the previous pages are saying in their heart, "Well, I don't know exactly what I'm supposed to do." Please understand this: The Lord has already deposited your destiny in your heart.

Many people have come to me and said, "You know, I don't know what I'm called to do in ministry."

It's really not difficult. First, Scripture says, "Whatever your hand finds to do, do it with all your might" (Ecclesiastes 9:10).

Secondly, what's in your heart? Someone might say, "I love working with children!" Well, get busy!

Someone else might say, "I like to teach." Then start preparing! Position yourself. If you have a desire in your heart, pay attention to that because Scripture says the Lord will give you the desires of your heart (Psalm 37:4). We have not realized that the desire for service—whatever form it comes in—is from God. He gave you the desire in your heart!

We've misconstrued that truth for years, even generations. We've treated this promise as if Jesus is a genie in a bottle, and if we want something, He's required to give it to us.

Allow me to give you a more accurate interpretation of Psalm 37:4: "The Lord will birth within you a desire according to the destiny He has placed within you, and because He birthed that desire, He will fulfill it."

Do you see it now? The Lord places a desire in your heart! And because He put that desire in your heart, He'll lead you to the

The Lord places a desire in your heart! And because He put that desire in your heart, He'll lead you to the fulfillment of that dream and vision.

fulfillment of that dream and vision. He will give you the desire of your heart. Faithful is He who called who also shall do it! (1 Thessalonians 5:24).

I've often heard believers express their longing and desire for the Lord as if they decided one day to be hungry for more of Him. No! God put that hunger in you. That's the grace of God. Count yourself blessed to have a passion for Jesus and pray for those who don't, because He's called you to be a forerunner in this hour.

Over the years, I've met many people who feel their decision for Christ was made entirely on their own and their desire to live for Christ is theirs, too. I don't know all of the reasons we're like this in Western culture, but please allow me to share some of the light I have on this subject.

We have a Greco-Roman mindset, feeling that we have to figure it all out. We have to quantify, and as we do so, we check off our "religious to-do list" to step into our destiny. We've been programmed to believe there must be a certain number of "steps" taken in order to attain a certain standard or level of spirituality.

Jesus just had only one. John 5:19 says, "Then Jesus answered and said to them, 'Most assuredly, I say to you, the Son can do nothing of Himself, but what He sees the Father do; for whatever He does, the Son also does in like manner.'" Jesus asserts His dependence on the Father and His distinct role subordinate to the Father's will and plan.

I love the way Jesus conducted His life and ministry! I'm going to share how some of this unfolded and became life-changing for me, because it's important for us to get past religious thinking and get to the reality of the Word. Some of us have been going around the same mountain for years, frustrated because we don't really understand why our attempts to accomplish His will for our lives doesn't seem to work. The reality is that every one of us has faced this same issue at some time.

What I'm endeavoring to share in this book isn't rocket science, but it is mystical. It's a road less traveled, and few will find it. The word mystical simply means mysterious which is a biblical concept. Our identity in Christ already demonstrates that we're a "mystical" people—new creatures.

This subject is rarely addressed to any extent because frankly, most of the Church walks in unbelief and darkness. I contend that there is more unbelief in the Church than in the secular world because we allow religious systems to keep us in bondage.

Jesus said we must learn to live and move and have our being in Him and live our life from heaven to earth where we're seated together with Him. As we develop and mature in our understanding of our true position in Him, we'll find we spend more time in the Kingdom realm—the heavenly realm—than we do here on earth.

Occasionally and at times, reluctantly, we engage the natural realm on an assignment from God, and then hasten once again to commune with the Lord in the extraordinary visual capacity that's become our natural inclination.

My good friends, Brother Sadhu Sundar Selvaraj and Brother Neville Johnson and I have talked about this issue many times. We recognize that there's a generation that's going to know what it means to access heaven and live from heaven to earth. That's a different type of Christian than the world has seen, but in this last generation, it's becoming a reality for many passionate souls.

One day, as the Lord and I were walking and talking about these revelations, Jesus would intermittently shift from a physical body to a Being of light. Every few steps He'd shift from His resurrected body into light and then He'd take a step or two and shift back to His resurrected body. Then, He'd shift to light again. He eventually shifted back and forth so fast that it became a blur and I couldn't tell the difference.

"I'm about to release a grace in this hour on My people," He said. "They will know what it means to live and move into other realms, and they will have a revelation that they truly are beings of light."

That's what God is doing now, and that's what you're being released to walk in. We think translation is something external that happens in an external realm. No, this realm is available to you because that's who you are!

The first Adam did this always. Moving from the spiritual to the natural was as normal to him as breathing. We've got to get back to that place because the world desperately needs, and is going to get, a demonstration of the Kingdom of heaven on earth. And the Lord wants you to be that demonstration! Let me say that again: Jesus wants you to demonstrate Kingdom life on this earth as it is in heaven!

> "And my speech and my preaching was not with enticing words of man's wisdom, but in demonstration of the Spirit and of power" (1 Corinthians 2:4, KJV).

We Must be a People of Faith before Reason

The first thing we must understand is that God opens our understanding. You can't figure this out or reason this out intellectually. God-breathed revelation can come no other way but by the Spirit of the Lord. Our friend, Julia Chmela from Vienna, Austria, is a worship leader but also studied theology in college. Julia realized that theology is nothing but a humanistic, intellectual denial of the supernatural God. That's an accurate picture of why the Church has become so stagnant in our day.

You cannot enter into the deeper things of the Kingdom of God with your intellect. Everything God releases must be spiritually discerned because the breath of the Spirit brings life. We must understand that we're called to be a people of faith before reason. You believe, and then you receive! You don't receive and then believe.

> Luke 24:45 says,
> "Then opened he their understanding, that they might understand the Scriptures …" (Luke 24:45, KJV).

This revelation must be God breathed. If you're like me, there were seasons when I'd read Scripture repeatedly yet glean little from what I read. Then, as I read it another time, it suddenly jumped out and came to life. That's God-breathed revelation! He has a specific moment of time when He wants to release revelation to you. This is how you get understanding of Scripture. Therefore, if you're a hungry people, you should spend more time in Scripture daily to receive insight and revelation.

In Luke 8:10, we need to pay attention to the phrase "Unto you."

"And he said, Unto you it is given to know the mysteries of the kingdom of God: but to others in parables; that seeing they might not see and hearing they might not understand" (Luke 8:10, KJV).

Who is this "you" He's talking about? He's talking to His disciples. There's a difference between followers and disciples. Disciples in Scripture are submitted to Jesus 24 hours a day, seven days a week, 365 days a year. Disciples went whenever the Master went. Being led by the Master, they did exactly what He directed. Disciples made Jesus the center of their lives. They ate what He ate, slept where He slept, and did what He commended them to do.

Those who only "followed" Him went where they wanted to go, ate where and when they wanted to eat, slept at home in their own beds and conducted their lives as they saw fit. Jesus was not their Master, their Rabbi. He was a prophet and a healer. Their lives did not revolve around Jesus like the disciples' lives did.

I've got to state this very strongly: There's a place of maturity in God where you can be entrusted by the Lord to make certain decisions. Those decisions, however, will never cross the line of scriptural precedence. Let me say that again. You can never cross the line of scriptural precedence and say, "This is God." That's why with any experience, you must go back to Scripture and say, "Father, I need understanding. What is this? What are You saying to me?"

I participated in a conference with a brother recently who made a statement that there are things that are "extra biblical, outside the Word, but still valid." As I thought about what he said, I knew it wasn't accurate. If it's of God, who is the Word, there's nothing outside of God. If it's God, it's from the Holy Spirit.

If you don't understand something yet, it doesn't make it extra biblical.

That implies it's beyond God or superior to God. No! There's no such thing. Every time you have an experience, go back to the Word, go back to the Lord and say, "Father, I need to understand this" because you're being commissioned not only to walk in this revelation, but also to communicate from Scripture the truth of what you're walking in. If you can't explain it, then be quiet and don't share it. This is critical!

On the other hand, somebody at one of our schools said, "My father was a Buddhist, and he died. I know he went to hell so I decided last night that I'd go back in time and lead him to the Lord, so now he's in heaven."

I explained to this brother that it doesn't work that way, as we don't make those kinds of decisions. Individuals must choose to follow Jesus before they die; we can't choose to "go back in time" to correct what you perceive as a mistake. You follow the Lord. You follow the leading of the Holy Spirit. You must be led of the Spirit.

God gives a grace period where He allows us to take certain steps to bring correction. We must, however, be careful to avoid following our own agenda. Submit everything to God. I'm saying this in love and because I want to caution you. Anything God wants to restore to the Church will have its foundation in the Word.

Even with a firm biblical foundation, some people will deny its veracity and some will go to the extreme. Both sides are wrong. Stay on the foundation. We're called to be people of the Word, like

You're being commissioned not only to walk in the revelation, but also to communicate from Scripture the truth of what you're walking in.

the Bereans. Scripture says God has given us to know the mysteries of the Kingdom.

> "And he said, Unto you it is given to know the mysteries of the kingdom of God: but to others in parables; that seeing they might not see and hearing they might not understand" (Luke 8:10, KJV).

The Lord has given this to us as disciples, but to the curious in the world, He gave parables. Remember, He only invested the revelation to the 12 disciples, but many others followed who only heard the parables. Become a disciple. Make Jesus your all in all, your magnificent obsession!

You Are an Ambassador of the Kingdom

For over 2,000 years in the church, we've for the most part, been blatantly unaware of the spiritual realm. The natural realm has captured our attention and become our reality. But when you're born again, your reality is not supposed to be the natural realm. Rather, our focus and place we set our affections should be in the eternal Kingdom. If we're citizens in heaven, we've have got to identify with the Kingdom of heaven.

You have a stewardship in the nation to which the Lord has called you because He put you here. Your stewardship here is to be as an ambassador of the Kingdom as that's where your citizenship has been established. We must hold loosely to the things of this world as we go about the business of the Kingdom.

The Lord gives tools to His ambassadors in the Kingdom of heaven. We speak with the authority of the sending nation and represent that nation in our actions. How we conduct our lives will speak louder than our words.

An ambassador receives certain tools by which to accomplish the task He was sent to fulfill. One of these tools is a lifestyle based on the dynamic Kingdom of heaven with all of its requisite abilities: its promises, authority, powers, etc.

A thought that challenged me over the years and provoked me to discovery was that an ambassador sent forth to represent the interests of their nation oftentimes flies home to receive instruction and input from the governing body that sent him. He will, at times, refresh himself/herself at home to remain firmly grounded in the understanding that they're representing their home nation and to keep them from becoming overly sympathetic with the nation to which they're sent.

I reasoned that if this was true in the natural conduct and affairs of an earthly ambassador, how much more should it be true of those who represent the Kingdom of heaven. As you'll discover in this book, that's exactly the case! We have the right and privilege of frequent visitation to our "home country"!

> "But the natural man receives not the things of the Spirit of God: for they are foolishness to him: neither can he know them, because they are spiritually discerned" (1 Corinthians 2:14, KJV).

Redeemed, natural human beings have the potential to discern and understand the spiritual realm. I say "potential," because again, God releases it and we must act on it. Our heavenly Father, who loves us more than we can comprehend, will not release things to His people that will destroy them.

At any time in our walk, we can choose to take a truth from God, go our own way, and destroy ourselves. But it's never in the heart of the Father to release a revelation that causes you to stumble and fall. His whole purpose is for you to grow up into Him and become like Him.

One of my favorite scriptures is what Jesus said in John 5:19: "Then Jesus answered and said to them, 'Most assuredly, I say to you, the Son can do nothing of Himself, but what He sees the Father do; for whatever He does, the Son also does in like manner.'"

A second verse that applies this truth to our lives is John 15:5b "For without Me you can do nothing."

> "I can of mine own self do nothing: as I hear, I judge, and my judgment is just because I seek not mine own will, but the will of the Father which hath sent me" (John 5:30, KJV).

This is the Son of God, the King of Glory saying, "I can't do anything by Myself." So, you see, we're in good company. He does only what He sees the Father doing! Is this then a problem for me since this means I have to see what the Father is doing? No! That's not a problem, rather, it's a promise! Jesus said, "The works that I do you can do also and greater" (John 14:12 paraphrased). This means that you can see what the Father is doing!

> "Verily, verily, I say unto you, He that believeth on me, the works that I do shall he do also; and greater works than these shall he do; because I go unto my Father" (John 14:12, KJV).

Religious tradition keeps us out of the Kingdom. I'm very strong and passionate when I talk about the religious system. I'm not against people and know that we've all been snared at one time or another and some of us remain snared in certain areas of our lives. What makes my blood boil is a religious spirit that keeps people in bondage. I hate that spirit, which is prevalent throughout the earth. Please understand that I'm not talking about people. I'm talking about a spirit when I talk about religion.

Matthew 23:13-14 says,

> "Woe unto you scribes and Pharisees, hypocrites, for you shut up the kingdom of heaven against men, for you neither go in yourselves nor suffer those that are entering to go in. Because you have elevated the tradition of the elders, theology of men above the Word of God, and keep people from entering the kingdom of God" (KJV).

That doesn't mean that every tradition is wicked or wrong, but it does mean that we must be aware of the snare of the enemy. Somebody once said, "Hold onto the Word of God tightly and the word of men loosely." Regardless of what stream of Christianity you've come from, hold onto the Word of God tightly, not the traditions of men.

These are simple foundational guidelines. We all need a strong foundation of the Word. Many are already walking in some measure of liberty in the realm of the spirit. To progress even deeper, we must establish a strong foundation in the Word.

Some readers are already experiencing visionary encounters and seeing the spiritual realm. God has given a grace to the Church right now and a new season of Kingdom encounter is available to every believer. However, many having these encounters have no biblical foundation on which to base their experiences.

Though the experiences have often been awe-inspiring and fun, it's time to move toward maturity and accountability in this area because the Lord wants to release you to a deeper extent than you've ever gone before. Even now, as I'm writing this, I see multitudes of angels with scrolls like graduation diplomas. The Lord is about to accelerate our "school of the Spirit" journey so we can "graduate" and be about the Master's business in this late hour!

Acts 10:41 says that Jesus was raised up on the third day and was shown openly, not to all the people but to witnesses chosen by God.

> "Not to all the people, but unto witnesses chosen before of God, even to us, who did eat and drink with him after he rose from the dead" (Acts 10:41, KJV).

To whom did He show Himself? Not to all followers, but to the disciples and the women who ministered to the disciples. However, this is available to anyone who belongs to the people of passion. Passion is the key!

THE FATHER'S IDEA OF RELATIONSHIP

> Isaiah 46:9-10 says, "For I am God and there is no other. I am God and there is none like me. Declaring the end from the beginning from ancient time what is yet to come, my purpose will stand, and I will accomplish all that I please."

The Lord declares the end from the beginning. I've been studying this for a number of years and have just been absolutely blown away by the scope of the revelation contained within the significance of this passage of Scripture. This truly is an adventure! As you dig into the Word and begin to discover every "first mention," an amazing and prophetic picture begins to emerge relating to the end times.

For those who don't understand what "first mention" is, let me explain. In the subject of biblical hermeneutics, there are a number of principles by which one may study Scripture. Biblical hermeneutics is the science of interpreting text in the Bible, including the "Literal Interpretation Principle," the "Contextual Principle," the "Scripture Interprets Scripture Principle," and as mentioned, the "First Mention Principle."

With that in mind, let's examine a few "first mentions" in Scripture to see how this applies to us. Again, the first mention principle is summed up in Isaiah 46:9-10.

In the beginning, when God created Adam and Eve, they had a relationship with Elohim. This was the Lord's intention and idea, not their idea. They enjoyed the privilege of daily walking and talking with the Lord face to face in the cool of the garden (Genesis 3:8). They had the mind of Elohim, the authority of Elohim, and the wisdom of Elohim.

God graced Adam to release the character of every living animal, each species of living thing, in all of creation. Ancient Hebrew tradition teaches that the Garden of Eden is placed outside of time. That means we're talking about a dimension that's not necessarily of the earth. Therefore, Adam could see and release creation from that place into the natural realm. He had the right to go back and forth between realms. If Adam was able to release this, he had to know the ecosystem in which each animal and creature had to exist. That means he could go anywhere on planet earth to establish that for which God had graced him.

The first Adam fell into error. It was Adam's fault. He was there watching Eve. What took place with Adam and Eve didn't happen in 10 minutes but came to pass over a long period of time as the serpent enticed and convinced them to question God. Do you get a thought after the devil speaks to you, and then act on it instantly? Few do. For most, a process of subversion and enticement eventually blossoms into full-blown action.

When we're part of the world, that process happens. But when we're in Christ, we get a "check" in our spirit that causes us to hesitate. It takes a while to break down people's identity and convince them to become who they don't want to be. That's what happened to Adam and Eve.

Adam and Eve's fall didn't happen on the sixth day or the seventh day. We know this because on the sixth day, they were still with God and the seventh day was a day of rest, which means there was no conflict. Adam and Eve's encounter with sin took at least 1,500 years because a day with the Lord is 1,000 years. So, sometime on the eighth day (eight meaning new beginnings), they have a new beginning and fall into temptation. Falling from that place of intimacy and grace, they moved from that realm of the spirit, and from being clothed in light. Before the fall, they didn't know they were naked because they weren't naked. They were clothed in light as with a garment, like God because He created them in His image. When Adam and Eve fell into sin by accepting the temptation, that clothing of light suddenly vanished, leaving them aware of their physical nakedness.

We can't allow that in our own lives. We're going to be clothed again in light as with a garment. When we were born again, God clothed us with light as with a garment, though we didn't realize it, because we're so engaged in the natural realm. If it's going to be as it was in the beginning, then God is bringing us back to this place of intimate relationship, because that was His idea of relationship. Our idea of relationship with Him has been limited: Accept Jesus, attend church, and read your Bible occasionally.

God's plan for relationship is far beyond that! You can choose to hang out with the King of Glory, spending time with Him anytime! Or you can ignore Him and speak to Him once a week.

"For through him we both have access by one Spirit unto the Father. Now therefore ye are no more strangers and

STEPPING INTO OUR IDENTITY

You can choose to hang out with the King of Glory, spending time with Him anytime! Or you can ignore Him and speak to Him once a week.

foreigners, but fellow citizens with the saints, and of the household of God" (Ephesians 2:18-19, KJV).

God's Purpose and Desire: That we Know Him Face to Face

Relationship is the Father's idea. Although Adam and Eve fell out of relationship, the second Adam—Jesus—came to restore that relationship. Jesus, the sinless man, shed His blood, died and rose again, making the way for us to enter back into relationship with God. From the cross until now, every believer has access to that level of relationship. Everyone! The disciples and the women to whom Jesus first appeared at the garden tomb enjoyed that intimate relationship.

We need to grasp something here. God's purpose and desire for you is that you know Him, face to face. These are the powers of the age to come in which Adam and Eve walked. This is available to anybody who loves Jesus now. In this life, not in the life to come! This is a challenge but we're growing into this and have stepped into it by faith.

Before they fell, Adam and Eve had longevity in their natural body because of their proximity to the King of Glory and His radiance. The more time you spend in the glory and presence of God accessing the place of glory, something happens in your mortal body!

Let me explain. Have you ever seen somebody slain in the spirit? Receiving the touch of glory makes something happen in mortal bodies. The physical body can't take it, so it short-circuits, then boom, they're gone in the spirit. The more time you spend in the presence of God, who is glory, the more you change and conform to that glory. It quickens your mortal body and does something at the molecular level that begins to change you.

Now, you embrace this by faith. I'm making a declaration that at the end of the age, where we now live, men and women of God will be transformed and step into glory for all eternity, instead of dying.

Walk and Model the Christian Gospel

The forerunners are beginning to access these things now. Scripture says in the last part of 1 John 4:17, "As He is so are you in this world" (KJV). Not as He was, a mortal man who died for us, but "as He is." As an eternal being, He's a being of light. In Him, there is no darkness, no sickness, and no lack. Scripture says, as He is, so are you.

You must make this choice. As you confess this truth over your life, you walk in it yourself. Don't go telling people, "I'm just like Jesus." No! Show them. Talk is cheap, so show them! Become like Jesus so they'll know that it's truth. Let's stop giving Christianity a black eye by mouthing off about things we don't live. If we live it, they'll recognize it.

Intrinsic in every human heart and spirit is a desire for the reality that God wants you to model. Scripture says that Christian Gentiles provoke the Jews to jealousy, not by shoving the Christian message down their throats, but by modeling the reality of Scripture. When they see that reality, they'll want it. So, become that light!

My wife, Reshma, shares in her testimony about how, as a young lady, she never wanted to get married (until she found the perfect guy, of course). She'd go to church and hear wonderful messages about how God is love, yet come home and see the relationships between her brothers and their wives. The contrast was horrible. "If that's love," she said, "I want nothing to do with it." They'd talk a good talk, but were whitewashed tombs. Inside, they were full of dead man's bones, void of power, void of presence, void of the reality of God. This is what we've given the world for far too long. It's critical that we model the reality of the Kingdom!

Get Hold of God's Promise – Defining the End from the Beginning

God declares the end from the beginning. He paints a picture for you to grab hold of and hold onto tightly! A key to remember is God's promise to Abraham, saying "I'm going to make your descendants, as many as the sands of the seas and as the stars of heaven." Wherever he walked through the desert in the Middle East, by day he saw sand and by night, he saw the stars. The promise was always in front of his eyes, even when he began to doubt. When the enemy flung those darts of unbelief, Abraham looked at the promise and kept the promise before him.

This is a promise from the Word of God, from God Himself. He said, "I declare from the end to the beginning, this is who you are, this is who I want you to be." If you put that promise in front of your eyes, meditate on it, chew on it and get it into your spiritual DNA, you become that promise. There's a process of walking the promise out, but it will never come to pass if you don't keep it in front of you.

In Genesis 28, we have another picture of God defining the end from the beginning. Though Jacob had a covenant from God, he used his intellect and strength to help God along the way, which didn't work. He ended up going away from his family.

Don't try to make things happen. Trust God! What I'm sharing with you is a promise that belongs to you. Exercise faith and agree with God to receive it. It never works to rely on your intellect and strength to make God's promise happen. If you'd like a good lesson in taking a wilderness journey, go for it. The wiser and better path is to wait on God. If He promises to do something, He's faithful to accomplish it!

"Faithful is he that calleth you, who also will do it" (1 Thessalonians 5:24, KJV).

We must move past the fleshly nature that tries to make God's plan happen. I understand passion, as I've been desperate for God since age 14 when I got saved. That passion continues to increase. At times people feel like saying, "God, why are you teasing me? You've said this is mine, and then you keep moving the cheese. And just when I'm ready to grasp it, You pull it back!" He's building a tenacity, passion and purpose in you. Never give up.

Jacob was on a journey, going back to the beginning and returning to the place of promise. The last word God had given Jacob was back with his family. We've all learned this lesson the hard way.

Until you do the last thing God said, He's not going to give you the next thing.

Now Jacob revisits the beginning because he's gone his own way and failed. He's in turmoil because he thinks Esau is still angry and still wants to kill him. Two supernatural beings in this world want to kill you: God and the devil. The devil wants to kill you and

STEPPING INTO OUR IDENTITY

take you to hell. God wants to kill your fleshly nature so you can walk in the powers of the age and go to heaven. You're a target!

As Jacob journeys home, he wrestles with his flesh nature, his natural man. Reaching Beersheba, he's tired from his journey and falls asleep with a stone by his head. I believe this is a prophetic picture of Jesus, the stone the builder rejected. The Lord has shown me that if your nightly meditations are on the Lord, especially as you fall asleep, He will communicate with you in your sleep. Sometimes that's the only time He can get some of us quiet enough to hear Him!

When you have what you might consider weird dreams, you honor God by writing them down and saying, "Father, instruct me. What are you communicating?" If you dismiss it as a weird dream, you're ignoring Him. It's possible that you don't recognize His voice, or don't have the level of intimacy you thought you did with Him. We've all learned how to tune people out, especially husbands, wives, and children. We ought to tune out the TV, not God!

In this place, Jacob laid down to sleep and dreams about a ladder set up on earth. Understand this because it's important: Adam and Eve were made out of the dust of the earth. Eve came out of Adam's side. When you see dust or earth in Scripture, think of flesh. This revelation will change your understanding when reading Scripture.

Jacob sees this ladder on earth extending to heaven, with angels of God ascending and descending. It's interesting that they're ascending first and then descending. One would think that if you saw a ladder from earth to heaven, you'd see angels coming down from heaven first. Think about that! The ministering spirits are sent forth to minister to those who are heirs of salvation.

"Are they not all ministering spirits, sent forth to minister for them who shall be heirs of salvation?" (Hebrews 1:14, KJV).

Recognize that angels first ascend to the Father on your behalf, and then return with an answer. The Lord wants you to know that He's already working on your behalf. Your angels, those assigned to you for life, are excited today because you're going to make the next step. I'm believing God and believing that the Lord Jesus is going to manifest His presence in your life today so that you can see Him.

Lord Jesus, we invite and welcome You and the angels around us. Tone down the frequency of the spirit realm so we can see You.

Our human eyes can't see this frequency of light, but our spiritual eyes can easily engage. All heaven has to do is tone down the frequency at which they resonate, and then the frequency of light is adjusted so our natural eyes can comprehend. We'll get into that later.

Genesis 28:13 says,

"And behold the Lord stood above this ladder, and said, 'I am the LORD God of Abraham, your father and the God of Isaac. The land on which you lay I will give you and your descendants'" (NASB).

Something about revelation releases a measure of authority to you. Wherever you are when you have an encounter with God, an atmosphere and measure of authority is released to you. You must inquire of God what you ought to do with that. With every encounter God invests something in you and wants you to begin to walk in that measure of authority. For Him, wherever the soles of your feet touch, is yours. Who initiates this? From where does the ladder go? From you!

After Jacob receives this revelation, he wakes up and basically says, "Wow, this is the house of God and the gate of the heaven!" What house of God is he talking about? There was one rock. The house of God wasn't a fancy building with nice lighting and speakers. Maybe the Church should go back to that revelation. Where His presence dwells, in you, is the house of God!

Walk in the Fullness of Who You Truly Are

You're the house and the gate of heaven. Grab ahold of this revelation! The Lord and His Kingdom are not "somewhere up there." He's in you!

> Jacob was afraid and said, "How awesome is this place! This is none other than the house of God, and this is the gate of heaven" (Genesis 28:17, NASB).

> "Do you not know that you are a temple of God and that the Spirit of God dwells in you?" (1 Corinthians 3:16, NASB).

You're the house and the door. How do you step into the spiritual realm? Since you're the door, it's not outward; it's inward. The Kingdom of heaven is found by stepping through the door. This is a picture of stepping away from the natural realm and into the realm of spirit. Most encounters you'll have will be inward, but inward is the gateway to **outward**. Since you're the door, let Him out! And let yourself—that being of light—out!

Be A Walking Open Heaven

Some years ago, I was ministering in a town in Maryland close to Washington, D.C. While in my hotel room I had an encounter with the Lord as He taught me an astounding truth. One moment

I was sitting in my room, and the next moment I found myself in the realm of the spirit. As I stood there, the Lord said, "Take that off. Remove that garment."

"Okay," I said, and began to remove what at first, I thought was my shirt. As I undid the first button, a blinding light shone forth! Startled, I dropped my hands away from my buttons and hesitated.

"No," He said. "Take the garment off." Hesitantly, I took it off.

When I finished, I was again startled and in awe at what I witnessed! I realized I was no longer flesh and bone, but was a being of light! I looked behind me at the garment and realized it wasn't my "natural" clothing as I first thought. The "garment" He had directed me to remove was my flesh, which was pretty ugly (just saying). Jesus said, "It's time My people learn how to walk in the fullness of who they truly are."

You are light! We need to connect with the reality and revelation of this powerful truth! How do we do that? I practice every day by doing what I did that first time Jesus revealed this truth to me. I see myself removing that garment of flesh to enable the real me—the new creature—being clothed in light to come forth. If you start practicing that today, you'll walk in it.

Decisions must be made every day: Are we going to be the house of God? Are we going to open the gate? Are we going to be who God created us to be as sons and daughters of light? Are we going to choose to walk in that realm or are we going to go about our daily natural life like we've always done? We can make these choices based on promises God has given. Other choices can't be made because they're not based on His promises. It doesn't work. I can't choose of my own volition, for instance, to go back in time to lead someone to the Lord.

My grandma on my mother's side was a five-foot nothing German. Mean as a pit bull, she would beat the tar out of people who crossed her, even at 92 years of age. She smoked like a chimney, cussed like a …well …a sailor would be embarrassed by her language! A bitter woman, she wanted nothing to do with Jesus. When she died, of course my mother was hurt and broken. As Mom traveled to Canada for the funeral, the Lord said, "No, let the dead bury the dead. You stay home."

I can't choose to go into hell to bring her out, as that's not scriptural. However, God can raise the dead and bring somebody like that back to life and while back in their body, they can hear the gospel. You don't have the choice to go into hell and bring somebody out. I can't choose to go into heaven, grab hold of angels and say, "Come with me," as we don't have that authority. With God-given promises, however, you have a choice. You can be more like Him, saying, "I can of mine own self do nothing…" (John 5:30, KJV).

32 years into my Christian walk, the Lord finally got through to me. For 32 years I gave God some of the most creative and amazing suggestions on how to answer my prayers. I've had some doozies! The funny thing is, He never answered me once in the way I suggested He should. It was 32 years of, "I don't think so."

I can't tell God what to do! He knows the end from the beginning and I'm here, in the moment, telling Him how to make things happen? I've learned, by the grace of God, to say, "Father, here's the situation, here's the need, this is the circumstance, and I thank You because You take care of all my needs according to Your riches in glory!"

God does things the way He wants to do them, and His answer has always been far beyond anything I could have imagined anyway. We're always in awe of His ways. We can't tell God what to do but instead can present our needs before God and thank Him for the answer. That's how to receive exceedingly, abundantly above all we can ask or think. If we tell God how to answer, it's not going to happen, but if we allow Him to have His way, He'll do amazing things.

You Are the Door

If we conduct ourselves with the understanding that we're to be a walking open heaven everywhere we go, heaven invades the earth through us. Through us heaven invades earth, creating a spontaneous combustion. Let me give you the New Testament paraphrase: Jesus said, "I am the door," and "nobody comes to the Father but through Me."

"I am the door of the sheep" (John 10:7b, KJV).

"Jesus saith unto him, I am the way, the truth, and the life: no man cometh unto the Father, but by me" (John 14:6, KJV).

If you're the Body of Christ and Jesus is the access point to the Father, and He's the door, then you're also the "door" and also have access to the Father. Paul said, "I walk in the spirit not after the flesh." Choose to walk in the spirit. It's your choice.

Psalm 27:8 says, "Seek My face, my heart says to You; Your face, Lord, do I seek." Christians often spiritualize these scriptures. One

If we conduct ourselves with the understanding that we're to be a walking open heaven everywhere we go, heaven invades the earth through us.

scripture says, "No man shall see God and live." Right?" Exodus 33:20 says, "And he said, 'Thou canst not see my face: for there shall no man see me, and live'" (KJV).

You can't build a theology based upon one scripture! In the mouth of two or three witnesses His word is established! (2 Corinthians 13:1).

18 different scriptures in the Bible provide examples of those who talked to Him face to face. Let me give you just a few:

- God ate food with Abraham in Genesis 18:8
- 74 men ate with God in Exodus 24:1-11
- Joshua and all Israel saw Him in Joshua 5:13-15
- Gideon saw the Lord in Judges 6:11-23
- David saw the Lord in 1 Chronicles 21:16-17
- Job saw the Lord in Job 42:5

These are just a few examples but there are more!

"And the LORD spake unto Moses face to face, as a man speaketh unto his friend. And he turned again into the camp but his servant Joshua, the son of Nun, a young man, departed not out of the tabernacle" (Exodus 33:11, KJV).

This is the flawed human condition. We take one negative and hang our hat on it without any understanding, rather than taking the overwhelming abundance of evidence to the contrary.

A more literal translation of Exodus 33 where the Lord spoke to Moses and said, "You cannot see My face and live," would be "there is no human being with Adamic DNA who could see the face of God and live." In other words, your flesh, the corruption within you, will be destroyed if you come into the presence of the glory of God.

A New Adam – Jesus Christ and the DNA of the Messiah

We have the new Adam—Jesus—we were born again into a new race, a new creation, and have the DNA of the risen Messiah within us. You can now "see" God face to face if you have that DNA. In the original Aramaic and Greek languages, 2 Corinthians 5:17 says, "All things have passed away, behold all things have become new." That includes your DNA. Your new DNA does away with generational curses of sickness. You have the DNA of the Messiah, who was never sick a day in His life as a human being, not to mention that He's the risen Lord! These promises continue throughout Scripture.

So, you contend, "I've got this DNA, this DNA destroys all sickness. Disease can't live in this mortal body and definitely cannot adhere to the spiritual man." Simply don't allow it! Most of us are sick because we allow it or are ignorant and lack understanding of the Word. Don't tolerate sickness!

Even now, there are going to be plagues coming on the earth and hideous things released that have never been seen before. No science will overcome them. But if you know who you are in Christ, they will never touch you. You'll be the answer for those who need the answer. You watch! Mark my words. Scientists will ask some of you for your blood because you never get sick. You have the blood of Jesus, the blood that cleanses you!

Psalm 27 says, "Seek His face. His face do I seek." 1 Chronicles 16:11 says, "Seek the Lord and His strength, seek His face continually" (KJV). What kind of God says, "Seek His face" and then says, "If you see Me you die"? A God of Love? We must all be aware of this scriptural truth: God wants our flesh to die and longs for us to return to that first state of INTIMACY. The only way to that intimacy is to crucify the flesh. We must continually recognize that we're dead, and our life is now hidden in Christ Jesus! The crucified life is the life of the Kingdom!

If we're in Christ, then we're dead, buried, and raised again. We died so we can see His face! Scripture says the angels want to look into the mysteries of redemption, yet they don't understand these things (see 1 Peter 1:12). Even now as I'm sharing this truth, angels around me are amazed by this revelation. They want to understand this because the whole concept is foreign to them.

We've used and handled the Word of God so lightly in a religious, non-approachable way, that we've come to take it for granted. God's Word, the Scriptures, are sacred and contain life. The Word becomes a gateway, a doorway into a new realm of life.

Scripture says that Jesus was the exact out-shining and representation of the Lord, the Father (see Hebrews 1:3). Study this powerful truth! People say, "We want Your glory, Lord." His glory is a person and His name is Jesus. Let me say that again. We cry out for the glory, which is good, but glory is a person and His name is Jesus. He's the outshining of God. You're already in Christ and already have access to His glory if you do what He does. He's stepping from one realm to another always, as seen by the millions being saved by visitation.

You have access. You have access. You have access. Some that have already had these supernatural experiences are now going to receive things from the realm of the spirit from which you'll physically bring back into this dimension. Guard that, as it's a sacred trust from God! If you steward what God gives you wisely, He'll give you more. Yet, if we become frivolous with that which is holy, we won't receive more.

A Reserved Manna for this Generation

I'm seeing in the spirit right now, loaves of fresh manna, the same food given to Elijah to strengthen him for 40 days. The Lord has this provision in reserve for His people in this hour. Those with the ears to hear in your spirit, you're going to bring this manna with you, to feel and experience supernatural strength come, even in weakened bodies, as God releases this manna to this generation.

Matthew 7:7 says, "Ask, and it shall be given you; seek, and ye shall find; knock, and it shall be opened unto you" (KJV). If you're seeking the face of God, seeking to walk in the powers of the age to come, desiring to honor God in these things, He's going to give it to you. However, in the original language it says, "ask and keep on asking." Don't grow weary in this, saying, "It didn't work for me," because it's not going to work for you, you work for Him! Keep going. Keep going. Keep going. He rewards those who diligently seek Him, not those who halfheartedly request of Him. Keep going!

The Glory of God Transforms You

Adam and Eve talked face to face with God before the stain of sin blinded their spiritual eyes. That's why we keep short accounts by the blood of Jesus, saying, "Father, forgive me if I grieved You. I repent." For centuries, the Lord told Israel to seek His face, but they took it symbolically and metaphorically, saying, "Lord, Lord, Your face we will seek." They established religious practices rather than making God approachable. Israel made God so unapproachable that they kept people from encountering Him.

Don't do that! They missed God face to face as the glory of God was revealed, and the time of Messiah through the face of

Jesus Christ. 2 Corinthians 4:6 says, "For God has shined in our hearts to give the light of the knowledge of the glory of God in the face of Jesus Christ." When you have an encounter with His face, you're encountering glory. Amen! You need this life-changing encounter.

The Lord manifested Himself in the flesh when Jesus came. He wants to manifest Himself in your flesh so that when men and women in this world look, they won't see you, they'll see Jesus.

Years ago, I was praying and said as I often did, "Lord, all of You, none of me. I want to be like Jesus." I've had that encounter before the throne of God in heaven too, expressing my desire to be like Jesus. Then, one day I read in Acts 4 where Peter and John were taken, thrown into prison and warned, "Don't again preach in that Name."

> "And they called them and commanded them not to speak at all or teach in the name of Jesus" (Acts 4:18, KJV).

I love that because they had been told, "Just be quiet and walk down the street" yet as they walked down the street, people were healed! They even carried the sick out into the streets and laid them on cots and pallets so that when Peter came by, at least his shadow might fall on any one of them (Acts 5:15, NASB).

The Pharisees said to Peter and John, "We can see you are unlearned and ignorant people, but we can also tell you've been with Jesus" (Acts 4:13). How could they tell they had been with Jesus? It wasn't through their eloquence but because the manifestation of the Spirit of God was present. They could see a tangible, visual manifestation of God's presence.

Remember Jesus on the Mount of Transfiguration when Peter, James and John saw that manifestation of transfiguration.

"Now after six days. Jesus took Peter, James, and his brother John, led them up on a high mountain by themselves; and He was transfigured before them. His face shone like the sun, and His clothes became as white as the light. And behold, Moses and Elijah appeared to them, talking with Him" (Matthew 17:1-3).

They were looking for a manifestation of His presence because they knew it would be a sign that the return of the Messiah was here. That's why I'm so excited in this generation. Jesus was once again clothed with light, talking with Moses and Elijah face to face. You can call that translation, visitation, or whatever you want, but the fact is, that's happening in this generation! They taught about that, saying that when this takes place, we're going to be changed to be like Him before He returns.

That's happening in this generation. In every encounter, a transformation begins to take place. The more you see Him, the more you're with Him, the quicker this acceleration of transformation takes effect. The world has never seen what's about to be sprung on them. Get ready because you're going to turn the world upside down. I've heard the most astounding testimonies of young people having these incredible encounters in these present days. Get ready, because it's going to happen to you.

GODLINESS – GOD-LIKENESS

1 Timothy 3:16 says,

"And without controversy, great is the mystery of godliness: God was manifest in the flesh, justified in the Spirit, seen of angels, preached unto the Gentiles, believed on in the world, received up into glory" (KJV).

We've understood godliness to be a conduct of character. If we say, "Oh, they're so holy and pious" what we really mean is,

"They're so religious and gag me with a spoon!" That's establishing protocols: you can't part your hair this way, you can't wear this, you've got to walk like this, speak like this, etc." And they have equated those things with godliness.

That's not godliness. It's foolishness! Great is the mystery of godliness. God was manifest in the flesh. He wants to manifest in your flesh, so pay attention. The mystery of "God-likeness" is that He'll manifest it through your flesh.

The justification for godliness is in your spirit. Seeing angels, preaching to the Gentiles, believing the Word, and being received into glory is a roadmap for you! The Lord wants to openly show Himself in your natural life and has enabled your spirit man to lead you in life. Your spirit is capable of leading because when you received Christ, His Spirit indwelled you.

"Preach unto the Gentiles" is an interesting phrase in the Greek and means share. It's more "caught than taught" as people learn more by watching what you do than by listening to what you say. Preach to the Gentiles and preach to those without Christ by modeling the reality of the Kingdom. They will see if we don't get sick, if we don't tire easily, if we never succumb to defeat, and if we're always blessed with abundance because we recognize our true source.

As God's people, we're not broke because our provision is in heaven. Our life is from heaven and the source of everything in our lives is the provision of heaven. Our citizenship isn't of the earth; therefore, we partake of the rights of our heavenly citizenship. Study Scripture because it provides understanding of what it means to be a believer. When it's modeled by us, it's believed on the world, and when it's believed on in the world, many are received up in the glory.

Let me express this truth another way: Scripture, like all of history, is a circle that tells the end from the beginning. Jesus, initially in heaven with His Father, came to earth, then returned to heaven. You can follow this circle pattern throughout Scripture. Consider this in light of 1 Timothy 3:16 which says, "It's a mystery, God manifested in the flesh, revealed himself and was caught up in the glory." It's a circle! That means that you always have access to Him.

Acts 22:14 tells us that God the Father has chosen you:

"And he said, 'The God of our fathers hath chosen thee, that thou shouldest know his will, and see that Just One, and shouldest hear the voice of his mouth'" (KJV).

Make this declaration: "I'm chosen!" You've been chosen to know His will, to see Jesus, and to hear the voice of His mouth. Then you'll be His witnesses to all men of what you've seen and heard. That's your commission! What you see, hear, and experience, which is part of seeing. What you hear is to be used as a witness to all. There's a great move of God taking place and it's about to explode!

Make this declaration: "I'm chosen!" You've been chosen to know His will, to see Jesus, and to hear the voice of His mouth. Then you'll be His witnesses to all men of what you've seen and heard.

Chapter Two

PASSIONATE FOR THE LORD

I again want to start this section with a declaration. As you declare these words, no darkness will come upon you or hinder you. Speaking and believing this statement is a step of faith and going forward is a decree you can use every time you position yourself before the Lord for increase.

> "From my position in Christ at God's right hand, I decree that I am loosed from the power and influence of the devil. I decree that all deaf and dumb spirits must go, and all spirits of spiritual blindness must go. Go now! Amen. I loose myself from all doctrinal error and all teaching that would hinder and block my relationship with God. I call for God's light to fill me to overflowing and dispel all darkness. I declare that I am light, just like my heavenly Father. I receive everything that the Lord has for me, without reservation. Amen!"

Your Birthright in Christ

Your birthright is something that belongs to you and is as natural as breathing. Some people say, "We want to make it second nature." No! Your birthright must be first nature. We want to put everything God has given us first, not second. We endeavor by faith to enter into the fullness of God's promises. We must consistently apply those promises in our life; one way we do that is by making a declaration as we just did. We make a declaration with our mouth because God created the world by words and has given us the same creative ability. We establish our life and our walk with God by what we speak.

Begin to Walk in the Realm of Expectation

Sometimes we make faith declarations where the theology is a bit lacking to say the least. Many worship songs are in the future tense. For example: "Oh Lord, I really want to see You," or "Oh Lord, I really want to know You." I can't sing those words. One song from the '90s was, "Open my eyes, Lord, I want to see Jesus." I can't sing that one either because it's future tense.

According to the Word of God, I already have a visual capacity, so I say, "You've opened my eyes, Lord, now I see Jesus." It's become a habit in my life to make declarations according to Scripture and make it in the "now" of my existence, not someday in the sweet by-and-by. When you ponder this subject, don't think, *Well, I hope by the end of the week...* No! It's yours right now!

Some who desire and learn are going to begin fading in and out from one realm to the other. If you experience this, you don't need a man teaching you, just begin to walk in it! It will become the norm for you. If some of you begin to disappear, don't be upset. Be excited!

I come before the Lord with expectation. Some years ago, the Lord told me there's a realm of the spirit called the "Realm of Expectation." It's the place of miracles where the fertile soil of the breakthroughs of God exist. You can live in that realm of expectation with daily expectation. Do you wake up expecting a visitation from God or do you get up and say, "Here's another day. Let's clock in and clock out." When you show excitement and expectation for revelation of the mysteries of God, you'll not be disappointed. We've got to shift the way we think.

You have Access to the Presence of God

Mark 15:37 says, "When Jesus cried out with a loud voice." This is when He finally says, "Okay, enough," and breathed His last. The Greek tense here is very instructive. When He breathed His last, "It is finished," it was like the same breath of God at the creation. When He breathed His last, there was a release of Ruach HaKodesh, the Spirit of God that created access for you into the Kingdom of Heaven. He said, "I have finished my goal. I have attained My goal. Bride, come forth!" That was the moment of birth, the moment of releasing and unlocking these mysteries for you. It was a creative act because the breath of the Almighty God was released.

He said, "Come forth," and breathed His last. After He said, "Bride, come forth!" it says, "Then, the veil of the temple was rent in two." If you study the tabernacle and the temple, you'll find a pattern for going to this realm of the spirit. The outer court, which is the court of the Gentiles, everybody, or we could say "followers" have access. The inner court is for those who have spent more time and worked harder.

There's a picture of a tree on the veil on the outer court. Not the terebinth, but a picture of a tree with the cosmos embroidered along the sides. It's a prophetic picture that, as you enter into this place, you access the dimensions of God in which very few walk. That's why Gentiles couldn't enter into that place—the Holy Place.

The Most Holy of All had the cherubim with a flaming sword, the same one that kept Adam and Eve and any other person from entering into the Garden of Eden. When Jesus breathed His last, that veil was torn, giving access once again into the presence of God. That's not only positionally or visibly—it's physically. You have access now, where you haven't had access before. That relationship reestablished the Genesis Chapter 1 level of relationship.

You Can Come Boldly to the Father

The Father has been speaking to me, and I'm excited. He says we're going to the children's room which means child-like faith is about to be released to you. God speaks to me, and maybe to you, with symbolism in Scripture. Pay attention to those things. God speaks to the minutest detail if you have eyes to see and ears to hear.

Jesus breathed, releasing that creative breath of God that tore apart the fabric between two dimensions, two realities. He says, "Now you can come boldly." Now you can come boldly! Now you have access to the Father. The Father says, "Come on back in, kids, I've missed you!" We can come boldly to the throne of grace. That doesn't mean kneeling down and praying, although that's part of it. But if you can receive it, you can actually go. I'll teach you how to make the connection. It's not hard to do and only requires a couple of easy steps.

Pursue God with All of Your Heart

Jeremiah 29:13 offers a key: "And ye shall seek Me, and find Me, when ye shall search for Me with all your heart" (KJV).

Haphazardly and half-heartedly seek God? No! God said, "Give it everything you've got! Pursue Me with all of your heart, and I'll be found of you." As you pursue God with all of your heart for what you don't see, He will run toward you as you take that step of passion. He just doesn't stand there and say, "Come on, you can do it. Come on!" When He sees that level of passion in your life, God runs toward you and tackles you. He's waiting for you!

I love the fact that the Lord has a passion for us that transcends and far exceeds anything we can think or imagine. His passion for you is beyond anything you've experienced. In this hour, He wants to embrace you with that passion.

How do you think the first century Christians could go into the coliseums singing, worshipping, and praising God in the face of death as the lions tore them to pieces? They didn't feel the pain; they saw the glory. Supernaturally, God shifted them away from the physical, natural realm. They went into glory worshipping God. Stephen, the first martyr, with eyes open, saw the Lord and didn't feel the stones as he transitioned into glory. A grace comes on you as you begin to engage the supernatural, spiritual realm.

You may be familiar with Neville Johnson or have heard him speak. Neville had a vision of Jesus leading a host of young believers to take a particular city in a nation. They had machine guns and were lined up to do warfare. The Lord stopped and said, "I need a martyr."

A young lady said, "Oh, oh, me!"

His passion for you is beyond anything you've experienced. In this hour, He wants to embrace you with that passion.

"Go," the Lord said. She took off running as fast as she could to be martyred for Christ and as she ran, they began to shoot. Neville said that as he watched this in slow motion, the bullet came toward her but just before impacting her, her spirit left her body. She was then standing with the host of believers, but now in the spiritual realm. They all moved forward together because that blood had been spilled. Now God had legal access.

God releases a grace. Do you know why some people fear death? First, they don't like pain, and secondly, they're not convinced of what lies ahead. People are afraid of walking into the realm of the spirit because they don't know that it's theirs or that it's biblical, and they don't want to be ostracized. The same principle applies to pain, fear of the unknown and fear of rejection. Don't be afraid.

If Jesus is your ultimate goal, your magnificent obsession, everything else disappears. You're not impressed with people's opinions, accolades, or snide remarks. You don't even hear it as you have one focus set before you—Jesus. That's why the Lord taught Abraham to set the promise before his eyes. When the devil comes in with his innuendo, seeds of doubt, accusations and condemnations, you don't hear it because you're focused. We've got to learn this! As you continue to practice, you'll develop the ability to stay focused on the truth and on the light, not be swayed by every wind of doctrine, opinions and distractions of the natural realm.

When I first started this journey, the Lord taught me, "Learn to see with your eyes closed. Learn to engage with your eyes closed."

I said, "Why, Lord?

"Because you've got to learn to close out distraction," He said. "You're not using your physical eyes anyway; you're using your spiritual eyes." As some know, with your eyes closed you can see in the physical and the spiritual, which is awesome. Notice that your spiritual eyes are not limited to 20-20. They can see around the world. He taught me how to see and interact with my eyes closed. Now I can see with my eyes open. Sometimes it's very interesting, yet sometimes it's very distracting.

Once I was ministering in a small church in Spokane and saw angelic activity in the room. I looked down to read Scripture and when I looked up, I went blank. I must have appeared like a deer in the headlights, seeing these angels suddenly doing handsprings at the back of the church! I thought, What is this?

"Lord, that's sacrilegious!" I said. "Angels don't act like that."

He said, "Have you not read in My Word that the angels rejoice when one sinner is saved?"

But I thought rejoicing meant more like saying, "Yay!" Oh, no! Their whole being is engaged in joy. Not simply joy with decorum—true JOY!

Looking at this left me dumbfounded, I lost my train of thought and didn't know what I was doing. Everybody watching said, "What's the matter? What's the matter?"

"Uh, well," I said, "I'll tell you what I saw."

When I shared what I had seen, one lady on the front row got up and left, saying, "God doesn't act like that." She never came back, but that's okay. You'd be surprised at the things God does. He has a tremendous sense of humor!

James 5:16 says, "Confess your faults one to another, and pray one for another, that ye may be healed. The effectual fervent prayer of a righteous man availeth much" (KJV). That could take a month of Sundays, but do you know what we do instead? We confess others' faults among us. "Let me tell you about Mike." Is it any wonder the Church is lost in the wilderness of doubt, unbelief and apostasy, when we speak about others instead of speaking about the King?

"Confess your faults one to another and pray for one another." Wouldn't it be interesting if those in the Church said, "I don't like that guy, I better pray for him." That's what the Word says to do. "You really offend me, let me pray for you." Instead, we say, "That guy really offends me, do you see what he did?" Then we tell everyone.

That's not what Jesus did. We've got to change the way we comport ourselves. He says, "You do all that so you can be healed."

Passion to Pursue Jesus and Walk in the Supernatural Realm of Glory

Let me take this to a different level. Do you really want to engage in the realm of the spirit, to see and to go in that realm? If you do, there's got to be a healing within you. If you're not seeing in the spirit, then something is wrong. If you're not walking in the realm of the supernatural, something is wrong and is causing a disconnect.

God wants to bring healing to that. He gave us the key: Confess your faults. You keep it pure. You keep it holy. You keep the application of the blood of Jesus. You keep short accounts on your own heart and pray for others instead of accusing others, and you'll be healed. Does the Word say the effectual half-hearted prayer of an unrighteous man availeth much? No! Here it is again: Passion. Everything you do for God must be done with passion.

Think about it. The devil's people are passionate. They're passionate to carouse, passionate to drink, passionate to commit fornication, passionate to cut your head off. They're passionate!

The Church is more like, "Okay ... Sure ... I love Jesus." Where's your passion? We've got to be a passionate people.

Here's what's going to happen to you. You're going to have an encounter with Jesus that's going to make you nuts. The world is going to say, "They're crazy!"

"You better believe I am," you'll say. "I'm crazy for my Jesus!" Have you ever seen a young couple in love? They're crazy! That's all they talk about and all they think about. It's their focus and their passion.

We need to be the same way. Many examples in Scripture demonstrate the proof of passion is pursuit. Don't tell me you're passionate and then sit on your blessed assurance and do nothing. That's not passion. Passion is always demonstrated in pursuit, which is not always physical. Passion overtakes you at times and you're overwhelmed with the feeling that wells up in your spirit and all you can say is, "Oh Lord, I want You, I love You, Lord!"

Reshma and I were talking about this recently. We're doing our normal routine throughout the day, when this passion rises in us and we say, "Oh Lord Jesus! I love You, Lord, I love You!" When you're in love with Jesus, you can't help being passionate because it wells up in you. It doesn't come out of your soul, but out of your spirit. Then it enters into your soul to affect your physical body.

The joy of the Lord is my weakness? No! The joy of the Lord is my strength! It's your strength! Think about the martyrs of the Kingdom who went to their death, as rejoicing became their strength. That's why they didn't feel the pain of passing into the eternal realm. They were like Supermen, Superwomen and Superchildren. The joy of the Lord became their strength!

When you're in love with Jesus, you can't help being passionate because it wells up in you. It doesn't come out of your soul, but out of your spirit.

I only have a couple of favorite scriptures, starting in Genesis 1:1 and ending in Revelation 22. The Word of God is the love letter from my Bridegroom. One of my favorite testimonies from God's Word is the passion of Zacchaeus in Luke 19:1-10:

> "Then Jesus entered and passed through Jericho. Now behold, there was a man named Zacchaeus who was a chief tax collector, and he was rich. And he sought to see who Jesus was, but could not because of the crowd, for he was of short stature. So, he ran ahead and climbed up into a sycamore tree to see Him, for He was going to pass that way.
>
> And when Jesus came to the place, He looked up and saw him, and said to him, 'Zacchaeus, make haste and come down, for today I must stay at your house.' So, he made haste and came down and received Him joyfully.
>
> But when they saw it, they all complained, saying, 'He has gone to be a guest with a man who is a sinner.'
>
> Then Zacchaeus stood and said to the Lord, "Look, Lord, I give half of my goods to the poor; and if I have taken anything from anyone by false accusation, I restore fourfold."
>
> And Jesus said to him, "Today salvation has come to this house, because he also is a son of Abraham; for the Son of Man has come to seek and to save that which was lost."

"Jesus entered and passed through Jericho." Do you realize in this hour across the planet, Jesus is entering into cities, and the power of God is present to heal and deliver them and set them free? Most people never avail themselves of it. This passage talks about a time Jesus was visiting with the Pharisees and Sadducees. Do you know why they're called Sadducees? They don't believe in the afterlife, so they're sad, you see? No resurrection for them!

Jesus, visiting the Pharisees and Sadducees, said the power was there to heal them. A lame man's friends brought him to Jesus on a stretcher. The religious leaders didn't receive the healing that was present to heal them, but the people of low estate, the commoners, came in faith and received healing.

Unfortunately, this happens frequently, when the presence of God shows up, yet the religious programs push Him away. I've watched this scenario time and again. God bless the pastors and other leaders, but we've been taught and educated in the school of religion, so we lift up the program above the presence.

When God shows up, something powerful can happen, so let God be God! Stop trying to fit Him into your program. He's a gentleman, so He'll leave. If you hit that place in worship when the presence of God comes, stay there! Forget the preaching, forget the passing of the offering plate, and stay in His presence. God takes care of the rest. If He says to teach, then teach, but follow His presence, not your program.

Jesus is entering but passing through Jericho. You, like Zacchaeus, can attract His presence. Even if He's decided, "I don't want to visit that city, they're hard-hearted and cold," you can attract His presence through your passion for Him. Zacchaeus was a tax collector whom people already thought was of the devil because he was a tax man—a rich, chief tax collector. We know he was a man of passion because one doesn't become the chief, CEO, or executive of the tax office without a measure of passion. He must be a diligent, hard worker, and a person of passion, which he was.

Zacchaeus had heard about Jesus of Nazareth, this miracle worker. Though that would pique anyone's interest, a desire was building in him: *I really want to see this guy! I'm curious, what does a miracle worker look like?* Have you ever wondered what a miracle worker looks like? Look in the mirror!

Zacchaeus thinks, *Wait a minute, He's coming to town. I'm going to run out there and see Him!* It's not the Pope, the President or the next movie star visiting. He's going to go see a King.

Though Zacchaeus has been successful in life, he's neglected spiritual growth, so he's short—physically as well as spiritually. He can't see through the press of the crowd but that doesn't dissuade him. He thinks, *I don't care about the limitations that are set upon me by birth, culture, or religious doctrine—I don't care!* I want to see this guy. He comes up with an undignified plan for the CEO of the tax office. He says, "There's a tree. I'm going to run ahead and climb the tree so I can see Him."

That's passion! Because he's saying, "I don't care what anybody thinks about me, I don't care how stupid I look, I want to see Him!" How badly do you want to see Jesus? How desperately do you want to walk in all He has for you? If you're passionate, you're not going to care what people think.

Zacchaeus runs ahead while Jesus is walking with His disciples, followers and crowds that want the next free meal and next round of miracles. The Bible says, "He lifts up His eyes." See? Passion lifts you up and elevates you above the masses. There will always be the masses, followers, and those that only want the next freebie. But something about passion lifts you up.

Jesus sees Zacchaeus and says, "Zacchaeus come down quickly. I'm going to stay at your house." He had planned to simply pass through town but changed plans when He saw passion in one person!

The passion of Zacchaeus caused him to receive exceeding abundantly above all he could ask or think. He just wanted to look, but now he's got a habitation. Historically, Jesus made Zacchaeus' home as ministry headquarters from that day forward. That's what passion can do!

We've been incredibly blessed being in places where passion for God has been overwhelming. We've seen coliseums with 10,000 people not just having church, but worshipping God with passion. That's why you see God moving so powerfully in certain nations. If you stick with that passionate pursuit of Jesus, you'll see heaven come to earth.

Prayer is foundational, of course, but prayer won't work without passion. Prayer fans the flame of passion in the people, then passion comes, and God says, "I'm going to stay with them." Then He releases those things in His heart for this generation. He's looking for people of passion. And that's you!

This outpouring is also happening in Africa. Certain places receive it, not because they understand it, but because passion has drawn God's presence. They want us to come and teach because they don't know why it's happening; they just know people are translating all over the world.

Prayer fans the flame of passion in the people, then passion comes, and God says, "I'm going to stay with them."

One Baptist pastor said this supernatural experience was happening to him. "Well, you know this is happening to me," he said. "I was in my office at church and then suddenly the Lord took me to America. I ministered to somebody, then came back, and it keeps happening. I can't tell my church about it or they'll kick me out."

This is the reality of the Kingdom of heaven. College students in Nigeria get together to pray and go all over the world at night to minister and then return the next morning to attend school. They're a people of passion!

God has infected a remnant people filled with passion, so He can invest into them the eternal Kingdom of heaven. That's what He's looking for, and that's why it's happening more with the youth at the moment. They're looking for a cause and they have passion. If you're over 20, start fanning the flame of passion. Okay, 25. God's not leaving you out. He's not leaving anyone out!

Let me tell you about my friend, Michael Van Vlymen. After I had written my book, *Gazing into Glory*, I was careful to not read certain types of books because I didn't want to parrot somebody else. If God's got me on the hunt for something in Scripture, I refuse to read other people's revelation because I don't want to parrot that. I'm an avid reader and have a large library. On airplanes coming to and from, I can read three or four books because I love to read.

While reading, I saw a book titled, *How to See in the Spirit*. I began reading it and I thought, *Man, this is really well written. He's made it. He communicates it all very simply and makes it achievable for anybody. I've got to contact this guy. I really like this.* Reading a bit further, I saw that he mentioned my name. *Oh no, I thought. I can't contact this guy now as that will look funny.* I finished the book anyway.

Seeing he had a second book titled *Angelic Visitations*, I bought it. While reading, I thought, *Oh man, this is great! I don't care if he mentioned my name or not, I'm going to contact him!* But there was no author's page so I was unsure of how to reach him. I remembered that in the first book he said something about Facebook so I searched for him on Facebook. To be clear, though I'm on Facebook, I don't like it as it's too invasive.

When I discovered that Michael had tried to "friend" me some time earlier, we connected and started talking. I was not only impressed with his writing, but was impressed with the character I heard when we communicated.

After inviting him to go with us to Perth to teach in our school, he said, "Well, I don't want to teach on seeing and going because you already do that. What else do you have?"

I said, "Well, how about spiritual warfare?"

"Oh yeah, I like that," he agreed. He sat down and wrote a book to bring with him to Perth. Now, I don't know if I like this guy or not as it seemed he writes too easily!

We got to know Michael who walks the walk. After Mike had learned to apply these simple principles, he was off and running. Mike and his wife, Gordana, are "normal" people but are translating and going places regularly. By applying these simple principles with faith and passion, you'll see God do the same for you. If you've already had amazing experiences, that's good, because you're going to have a lot more!

Chapter Three

YIELDING TO THE PROCESS

I sense a shift, not only in the atmosphere, but in what God wants to accomplish. That shift is going to be a part of an acceleration. I saw a gift from the Lord— packets of light. Angels are going to impart these packets of light to those who will receive the gift. If you want this gift, tell the Lord, "I receive it, Lord." As you receive that packet of light, there's going to be an unpacking even while you sleep, along with an acceleration of this process.

Resounding in my spirit is, "Put running shoes on! The finish line is in sight and there's not much time." Though I don't know if that means a year or 10 years, I do know that we—God's remnant people—must be about the Master's business.

When the Spirit of God says what Jesus said, "When I come, will I find faith in the earth?" you must determine that He'll find faith in at least one individual—you! It's time for us to do the work and be about the Master's business. A grace is coming for that.

We not only have to model the Kingdom of heaven but must model the character of Heaven. Far too often we witness not the character of Christ, but the inflated ego of man. I learned that lesson as a young man working at Trinity Broadcasting Network (TBN). Attending Bible College and working at the television studio in the evenings provided quite an education!

One of the guests I had the pleasure to meet was Dr. Richard Eby, author of *Caught Up into Paradise*. A medical doctor who lived in Chicago where it's frigid cold in the winter, he was retiring and moving to California where it's sunny and warm. While throwing out cardboard boxes from the balcony of his second story home, the rail on the balcony broke as it was rotten. He fell and landed on a rock at the bottom, splitting his skull wide open.

Dr. Eby said, "Gray matter was all over the ground." His brain came out of his skull, and he was dead. When the ambulance arrived, they saw the mess and said, "He's dead." Scooping up his brain, the paramedics pushed it back in his head along with the debris. After they put him on the stretcher, the Lord sovereignly brought him back to life.

While Dr. Eby was dead, he visited heaven and experienced a profound encounter with the Lord. It was evident that Dr. Eby had been in the presence of the living God because he carried that atmosphere with him. In the early years of Christian television, the major difference I saw in those who had a true encounter with God was that their character reflected it.

Betty Malz wrote *My Glimpse of Eternity*. When Betty's appendix burst inside her, nobody knew it, and even she thought it was simply a stomachache. With the poisons released into her system, she died. After being caught up into Paradise, she returned into her body. When Betty appeared on the program, she wasn't merely telling about an experience, she carried the character of the Kingdom.

As I watched guests over my three years at TBN, some people would say they had these extraordinary experiences, yet their life and character didn't show it in the least. I asked the Lord, "Father, what is this?"

"Be careful of deceiving spirits," He said. Some people saw what captured people's attention and started pedaling false testimony.

I'm telling you this because in this hour, you must walk with keen discernment. If you hear people giving glowing testimonies without a reflection of the character of the Kingdom in that testimony, stay away! Don't be sucked in only because it's supernatural, but look for the character of God. To walk in translation by faith, you must reflect the character of the King and be a people of humility, or you won't progress.

My prayer for you is this: If you're not going to walk in humility, I pray that God doesn't release this revelation to you because it will destroy you. He isn't imparting revelation for any of us to build our own kingdom and make a name for ourselves. No! We build up the Kingdom of heaven and His Name. If anything we do points to us, we're wrong. We must always point to Jesus.

The Lord gave me a key as I began to study this revelation and press into the process of developing, understanding and walking in it: My ceiling can be your floor. It's taken me 16-20 years to walk in these revelations, but it's not going to take you 16-20 years.

My dad has made this same statement for years. When my dad was saved in October 1973, I saw the change. After seeing a supernatural transformation in him, I knew God was real, so I went into my room and accepted the Lord the same day. My father went into the ministry and gave away his businesses. He didn't sell them, but gave them away to enter full-time into ministry. He worked behind the Iron Curtain for many years before the wall came down and for many years thereafter.

He'd often say, "My ceiling, the highest point I came to in my walk with God, is your floor." What does that mean? Where I leave off, you continue. That which is being deposited into you as you read, study and receive revelation, is your starting point. You're not starting back where I started. My ceiling is now your floor. Receive that by faith because the launching pad is on a higher plane. The altitude is low where you walk in meekness. You're meek and lowly, but God is releasing the ability to reach the stars!

This truth becomes evident in Scripture. While in Jericho, blind Bartimaeus heard that Jesus was passing through and had the passion to say, "I'm staying here!" When Bartimaeus, who had been blind since birth, heard about this miracle-working God, hope sprang forth in his heart (Mark 10:46-52). If you hear about this miraculous process where you can be healed, wouldn't that grab your attention too?

As Bartimaeus meditates on this idea, hope springs up and he becomes desperate as a passion is birthed in his heart. One day he hears a commotion coming down the street. Wondering what's happening, he grabs the people and asks, "What is it? What is this?"

Someone says, "It's Jesus of Nazareth!"

"Jesus, son of David!" Bartimaeus yells. "Have mercy on me!" They had just told him that Jesus of Nazareth was coming, so where did he come up with Jesus, son of David? His desperation and passion unlocked revelation!

Your passion to know God and to walk in the Kingdom is going to release revelation to you too, but like we see with Bartimaeus, passion also promotes persecution. Everybody around him was saying, "Shhh! Be quiet!" We do things decently and in order (in our church) on this road.

He cried out louder, "Jesus, son of David! Have mercy on me!"

Jesus stopped. Though multitudes of followers and disciples crowded the streets, the cry of passion arrested His attention. Jesus stopped and said, "Bring him here."

Suddenly, those who persecuted him and shushed him now became his best friends. "Oh brother, the Master wants you. Let me help you."

Be careful! Those that mock and ridicule you and claim, "This isn't God" sing a different song when you connect with God. All of a sudden, they slide up to you and become your best friends. Stay away from that! Have compassion on them, love them and pray for them. Show them by example, but don't let them grab hold of you and cling to you. Be a leader.

Blind Bartimaeus stands up, throws off his mantle and moves toward Jesus. Here's the other facet of passion: When he was a child, he had to go before the Levitical priesthood who examined his eyes and determined, "Yes, you're blind. Here's your license to beg," and gave him a special garment or mantle that signified that he was blind. That was his only means of surviving in that world. That special garment enabled him to beg legally. Yet desperate and sold out, Bartimaeus said, "All or nothing!" and moved toward Christ.

Passion says, "It's everything or nothing. I'm going all the way. If it kills me, I'll still praise You, God. I won't quit until I've attained that for which You've been chasing me."

Jesus asked Bartimaeus, "What is it you want?"

"Lord!" He said, "I want to see!"

Notice the Lord didn't say, "Let me call for the elders of the church, let us anoint you with oil, let me spit in the dirt and make mud," all of which are valid. He said, "Be it done to you according to your faith." Receive. We don't have to beg for healing, our faith releases it to us. The key is passion and being sold out to God regardless of the cost.

Immediately, Bartimaeus' eyes were opened and he began to praise and worship God. What happened next? He began to follow God. I love that. He began to follow God.

> "Then Jesus answered and said to them, 'Most assuredly, I say to you, the Son can do nothing of Himself, but what He sees the Father do; for whatever He does, the Son also does in like manner'" (John 5:19).

It's much easier to walk this walk with God when you can see. It's much more fun and interesting too! Sometimes people say they're "on a journey with Christ," but journeys can be boring. I'm on an adventure with Jesus. It's new every day, and it's a blast as you never know what He's going to do! That's why you live with excitement and expectancy.

Here's what Jesus was saying: The word "blindness" in this passage of Scripture means, "to be puffed up with pride, to be obscured with smoke." His pride kept him in blindness just as your pride will keep you in spiritual blindness. You must come before Him with a humble heart, be teachable and recognize your desperate need of Him. You can make this happen by going back to square one and repenting. I've heard testimonies concerning this subject, and some teach that before they allow people to engage in the deeper things, they must do some spiritual introspection, deal with issues of the heart, and repent.

YIELDING TO THE PROCESS

Don't be quick to say, "Yes, Lord" out of the emotion of the moment. It honors God more if you count the cost and say, "I'm not ready, Lord," than if you instantly say, "Yes, Lord," and don't follow through.

You don't come to God full of dead works. Instead, come to Him broken and in humility as He can work with that. We've got to die to the rudimentary elements of this world and learn to count the cost of commitment. I've watched Jesus walk into meetings and weep with a broken heart because people make a glib emotional commitment and never followed through. That breaks His heart and we can't be like that. When we give our word, we must keep it. Don't be quick to say, "Yes, Lord" out of the emotion of the moment. It honors God more if you count the cost and say, "I'm not ready, Lord," than if you instantly say, "Yes, Lord," and don't follow through.

Some business owners and pastors know exactly what I'm talking about. Pastors of churches know this as well. Some say, "Pastor, I'm called to this church. I'll do whatever you need." Then, when the pastor doesn't recognize the profound, wonderful gift they are, they wander off to another church. We don't always know about this as pastors don't usually speak about it, but I've watched this for years.

WE SEE THIS DEMONSTRATED IN THE OLD COVENANT:

In the year that King Uzziah died, I saw the Lord sitting on a throne, high and lifted up, and the train of His robe filled the temple. Above it stood seraphim; each one had six wings: with two he covered his face, with two he covered his feet, and with two he flew. And one cried to another and said:

"Holy, holy, holy is the Lord of hosts;
The whole earth is full of His glory!"

And the posts of the door were shaken by the voice of him who cried out, and the house was filled with smoke.

So, I said:
"Woe is me, for I am undone!
Because I am a man of unclean lips,
And I dwell in the midst of a people of unclean lips;
For my eyes have seen the King,
The Lord of hosts."

Then one of the seraphim flew to me, having in his hand a live coal which he had taken with the tongs from the altar. And he touched my mouth with it, and said:

"Behold, this has touched your lips;
Your iniquity is taken away,
And your sin purged.'"

Also, I heard the voice of the Lord, saying:
"Whom shall I send,
And who will go for Us?"

Then I said, "Here am I! Send me.'"

And He said, 'Go, and tell this people:
"Keep on hearing, but do not understand;
Keep on seeing, but do not perceive." (Isaiah 6:1-9)

It says, "In the year that king Uzziah died, I saw the Lord." Many say that no man can see God and live. The key is found in the story of King Uzziah.

King Uzziah was crowned king at the age of 16. He was untested, untried and concerned about managing the kingdom. He threw himself on the Word of God and had it read in the courts. He said, "We must toe the line and must follow the precepts of the Word of God." Until his 40's, because he honored God, God prospered him in everything he did. When King Uzziah was about 44, foreign kings came to marvel at his riches and cities he'd built, and pride crept into his heart. He offered incense up to God, something he was not allowed to do. He eventually became a leper and died. Isaiah 6 could be read like this: "In the year that pride died, I saw the Lord."

My heart is heavy for the corporate Church worldwide. We see far too much arrogance, haughtiness, a mean mentality and very little of "God, we only want to lift You up." That which is coming upon the earth is coming to help God's people become a broken people. Persecution, testing and trials break God's people. A broken and contrite vessel, He doesn't despise (Psalm 51:17). In that place of brokenness, you begin to spring forth into the fullness of your calling. I can't reiterate this enough.

When I said, "My ceiling is your floor" earlier, that floor you walked on came at great cost. I faced years of brokenness, testing and trials, and humility, and I have lost everything I've owned a number of times. I'd do it all again in a heartbeat for the intimacy I now enjoy with Christ. Anything I could've wanted in this world is nothing compared to that. My passion and heart is to lift you up to walk in His fullness. I encourage you again to keep your heart, guard your heart, for out of it springs forth issues of life.

> Keep thy heart with all diligence; for out of it are the issues of life (Proverbs 4:23, KJV).

The word "issues" means "boundaries." You establish the boundaries of your destiny by the heart attitude in which you walk. That's why you must guard and keep your heart. Do you want to expand your tent pegs and have greater influence as it says in the Old Covenant? (Isaiah 54). Then, keep your heart, because out of it proceeds the boundaries of your life. If you get puffed up, you'll crash; If you walk in humility, you'll prosper. This is a Kingdom principle. Learning to walk in translation isn't so we can hang it on our belts and say, "Look at me." It's so we can say, "Look what God has done."

2 Corinthians 10:4 says,

"For the weapons of our warfare are not carnal, but mighty through God to the pulling down of strong holds" (KJV). What warfare do you believe we face? Jesus Christ came to earth and lived a sinless life, shed His blood, died on the cross, and said, "It is finished."

He won the victory. Right? What victory are you trying to win? Are we shadow boxing? Are we reliving wars from the past as they do through historic re-enactments in America every year, like the Civil War in Gettysburg? You don't have to do that! There's one more war you must win and that's casting down imaginations and everything that exalts itself against the knowledge of God and bringing every thought captive to the obedience of Christ (2 Corinthians 10:5). That's where the war is. "Out there" it's been won, but you're going to have to win the war "in you."

You establish the boundaries of your destiny by the heart attitude in which you walk. That's why you must guard and keep your heart.

When you're faced with the movement of either light or darkness in the world, what you are inside determines how you walk "outside." It changes everything when we know we've won, know we have authority, know we're part of the Kingdom of heaven and know that the kingdom of darkness has no hold on us. I can walk according to that understanding and agree with it every time the devil comes at me with condemning thoughts like, *You're no good, you're not good looking enough, you're too fat, too skinny, too short, too tall, or you don't know enough words.* You must cast those lies down. You know the truth. Those condemning thoughts may be accurate in the natural world, but in the realm of the spirit, you're complete in Him. Therefore, don't receive that garbage. Cast it down!

It took me a long time to walk in what God had released to me because at that time I didn't understand where the real battleground was. I was binding the devil and doing every-thing I knew to do, but nothing happened. I remember in the past binding the devil for all I was worth, but I wasn't seeing the breakthrough. I felt this spiritual warfare stuff, so I was going for it. The Lord got my attention and said, "It's not the devil."

"What Lord?" I asked.

"It's not the devil."

"Lord, who is it?"

"Well, it's not Me."

"Well, who is it then?"

"It's your flesh."

90% percent of life battles are due to your flesh being in the preeminent position. It's not even the devil! Finally, I got it. When this Scripture (2 Corinthians 10:5) became real in my life, I started dealing with it seriously.

Did you know that your flesh has a voice? It speaks always and is often confused with the voice of God. Your spirit has a voice, your soul has a voice, the devil has a voice, and God has a voice. That's a lot of voices! Are we hearing voices? Yes! We're hearing voices. We've got to learn how to discern the difference between the voices we hear. For many years, I didn't understand the difference.

A Burning Passion

In 1986, I was a youth pastor at Cornerstone Church in Mountlake Terrace, Washington. At this time, a burning passion came into my heart, and I became so desperate for God that I thought I was going to die. I thought, *If I don't grab hold of God, I'm going to perish!* I'd go up to the church where we had youth church and for 8-10 hours a day, I'd shut and lock the doors to be alone with the Lord. I'd turn on the sound system, grab the microphone, sing, worship, and cry out to God all day long. "Lord, whatever it takes," I'd say, "I want to know You!" This went on for weeks as I couldn't get free of this compelling desire and was consumed with desperation for the living God.

This all-consuming desire was a grace. That grace would lift when I'd go back to the regular workday world and see all hell break loose. It seemed like every demon in hell would say, "Hey, we're going to have fun." For months, my whole world would crash and burn, and I'd come out of that season staggering like I had been beaten to a pulp. But then this grace would rise up in me again. I'd go up to the church, close the door and start crying out to God.

I heard the voice of my flesh saying, "Shut up already!" When I heard it, I started laughing, as I couldn't help it. It was the first time I recognized the voice of my flesh. My spirit was crying out for God, but my flesh was saying, "NO! NO! NO!" This continued for three years and at the end of those three years, I had lost absolutely everything. It took seasons of brokenness in my life to get rid of the voice of the flesh and yield to the process through which God wanted to take me.

Many would approach me and say, "Brother, I'd give anything to have what you've got."

"Oh really?" I'd say. "Let me pray for you." Then I'd pray, "Kill him, God, he wants this too."

I have a son and daughter from a previous marriage. During this season, their mother took both of my children when she left me to be with another man. Because I desperately loved my children, I felt crushed and broken. Though broken, I was free. The Lord had answered my cry as I had prayed, "Lord, whatever it takes for me to know You!"

Coming to the end of myself, I had nothing left but a little suitcase and a tiny, beat-up old car. I had never felt so light and free with a revelation of the love of God. He said, "I heard you." God doesn't agree with divorce, but that brokenness that came through my divorce changed everything in my life.

I took a month off and went to a friend's house in San Angelo, Texas which is in the middle of nowhere. You have to be moving in that direction to even hit that town because it's not on any beaten path. I parked there for a month and would spend the entire day and half the night in prayer and seeking God.

On April 17, 1989, at 1 a.m., I was up at the church praying, worshipping God, and pouring myself out to Him. I believed at this point that I could never be in ministry again because of the divorce as that's what I'd been told. I resigned myself to that reality and had peace in my heart. "Okay, Father," I said. "If that's it, it doesn't matter. I can still follow You."

I saw Jesus walk in through the back wall. For years I had been told, "He doesn't do that!" Oh, but He does! He walked in with an alabaster jar full of ointment, walked up to me and poured this ointment over my head. It felt like hot honey, not a painful hot, but a cleansing hot. I was undone!

I jumped in my car and drove to the pastor's house at 1:30 am. "Get up! Get up!" I said. "I just had an encounter with God!"

After I explained what had happened, he said, "Well, you're supposed to pray for people tomorrow."

"No!" I told him. "You know I can't do that." I thought I couldn't pray for people because I had gone to the "Almost-of-God Bible College" which told me I couldn't. My pastor friend, however, wouldn't hear of it.

The next day at church he said, "Bruce had an encounter with Jesus last night and was given an anointing. It's a healing anointing for spirit, soul and body. Everybody, come and line up."

After everyone in the church lined up, I said, "God, You know I don't want to do this. Forgive me but You did teach me that when I'm in the church, I'm under authority." I walked up, and didn't even get to lay my hands on the first person, when they dropped to the ground. I'd never seen that before! Boom! Every single one of them dropped and had an encounter with God.

The Lord said to me, "Did I not tell you, the gift and calling of God is without repentance?"

"Yes, Sir," I answered.

"Don't you ever put My blood on trial again and say it's not sufficient," He said.

Don't ever be afraid to step out in faith. Even if you fall, fall forward into your destiny, not backward into doubt. This is what life is all about. It's a process.

"Yes, Sir" I said. For the next four or five years, I was in God's "secret service." I wouldn't do anything unless I specifically heard God say to do it, which set the course of my life.

I don't do anything unless I hear Him say, "Do it." Am I perfect at that? Of course not, but I get better every time. Whenever there's an "Oops," there's also an "Amen" because it's part of a learning process, and God is gracious. Don't be afraid to make mistakes. Only one mistake would hinder you for the rest of your life: not trying. Don't ever be afraid to step out in faith. Even if you fall, fall forward into your destiny, not backward into doubt. This is what life is all about. It's a process.

This experience birthed a pursuit in my life and heart of knowing Jesus face to face with intimacy. It started in 1986 with a desperate cry of passion that continued until 1999, when the Lord said, "Translation by faith." When He started unlocking that revelation for me, it left me undone, which I still am!

People ask, "Have you had another experience?"

"Yes," I say.

"What is it?" they ask.

"None of your business unless God tells me to share it." You'd better do the same, only speaking when spoken through. You're a mouthpiece for the Kingdom. Do what He tells you to do. That's difficult for some Christians to grasp, but it's going to be a life and death decision in this hour. Please understand the seriousness of what I'm saying: Life and death.

Following God's Voice

In my father's ministry behind the Iron Curtain, they couldn't announce the meetings or the KGB showed up and threw you in prison. Most who experienced imprisonment didn't get released until the Berlin Wall came down and Communism was broken. The first time my dad went behind the Iron Curtain, they came into the town and had to give their passports to the hotel desk clerk. They couldn't go anywhere without signing out, and when they did, they'd be asked, "Where are you going?" Knowing exactly how long it takes to get from here to there, they'd clock people and know where they were going. If you stopped for any reason, they'd know and they'd watch you.

My dad went into his room and started to speak to his two companions. "So, where do we …" he said, when his friends cut him off.

"Shhhh," they said, quietly showing him the lamp where a microphone was hidden. They pointed out another hidden microphone on a picture frame and other microphones throughout the room. The KGB had bugged the room. These three men in three different rooms took out a little cassette player and played the gospel of John, then went outside the hotel.

"Okay, what are we doing?"

"Well, we have a meeting tonight."

"Oh really, where?"

"We don't know."

"What? How do you know we have a meeting?"

"The Spirit of God told us."

"Oh, okay. What do we do?"

"We're going to leave in 15-minute intervals."

They said to my father, "Ed, you go north, then go west, then go east."

"Then what?" he asked.

"Be led by the Spirit until you get there."

That's being led by the Spirit 101 in a Communist country! Your life depends on hearing God's voice.

Though terrified, Dad started walking. He walked for 10-20 minutes, not knowing where he was going, until he came to a "T" in the road. He said, "Lord, if You don't tell me, I'm gonna turn around and find my way back." Feeling a nudge to go left, he went left. He walked around a curve, turned the corner and came into a huge plaza filled with soldiers and KGB.

Back then, in the Soviet Union, everybody dressed in dull grey, so they all looked alike. Here comes an American wearing bright colors. *Oh, dear God! Dad* thought. Petrified, he kept walking. *Maybe they won't notice me*, he thought, walking right into the middle of the formation. Sweating profusely, he continued walking, went down an alley, then leaned against the wall. "Oh, Lord," he said. "I don't ever want to do this again."

Hearing footsteps approaching, he thought, *Oh no, they're coming after me!* Continuing further down into this alley, after 150 yards he realized the alley had come to a dead end so he was stuck. Hearing footsteps coming, he thought, *Oh no! What can I do?* Seeing a spiral staircase nearby, he thought, *Maybe if I go up there, they won't see me.* He climbed to the top of the stairs, yet still heard footsteps coming. Finding a door at the top, he knocked, hoping that whoever was inside might let him in. When the door opened, one of his friends greeted him. "Good, you made it!" he said. "Come on in."

My dad spent 15 years walking by faith like that, where his life depended upon his ability to hear the voice of God and be led by the Spirit. We're coming into those days again, only now, God is releasing tools to this generation that they didn't have before. We're going into the enemy's camp in the Spirit to see the strategies of the enemy, then return with specific instructions.

God is going to physically take you there supernaturally. We're going to receive strategies from the throne room of heaven through prayer and by literally going places to receive something to bring back.

What God is doing in this generation is unprecedented. We're called to walk in this revelation, but we must have the foundation of humility to operate in it. Be always aware of this and keep one another honest.

Remain Teachable

Many years ago, while ministering in a church, someone approached me and said, "You're pretty haughty and arrogant, aren't you?"

It shocked me. That hurt.

Wounded by this accusation, I went to my dad and said, "This is what they said about me… Is this true?"

"Well," Dad said. "Kind of." I went into my prayer closet, pulled the covers over my head and cried out to God. Sometimes you don't recognize things in your own life. I didn't recognize arrogance or haughtiness. None of us see our blind spots. Thank God for a father that was honest with me. I'm thankful for the person who pointed out my blind spot. Bless him, God! Though it hurt at the time, I'm thankful, as by speaking those stinging words to me, that person was being a true friend.

Get ready for correction. Your shepherd should be able to approach you, speak to you in love to address areas needing correction without you throwing a fit, raising a ruckus and spreading evil reports. If you genuinely want the things of the Kingdom, you will remain teachable.

Translation by Faith

In 1999–2000, I woke up one morning when God asked me a question. "Can a man be translated by faith?" I'm not normally a morning person and no longer get up at "zero dark thirty" which I did for many years in the military. I normally wake up about noon, the crack of noon, mind you! Five cups of coffee later, as I was lying in that bed in a half-asleep, half-awake state, the Holy Spirit spoke to me. This is when He often sneaks up on me because I'm not interfering.

"What's that?" I asked. Reasoning that if He's asking, it must be possible, so I said, "Well, yes, sir. I believe so."

"Good," He said. "Prepare!"

Shocked, I said, "What?" Pulling the covers up, I sat up. "Lord," I said. "How do I do that?"

"I just told you," He said. "By faith." Then His presence left.

I sat there scratching my head and mumbling. I knew the story in Scripture about Philip and the Ethiopian eunuch, hadn't thought about Enoch, and other things weren't clear in that moment. I felt confused. *What kind of a message is this?* I wondered. Then I started thinking, Was that really God? I mean I had some wicked pizza last night, so was that really God? I walked around in a state of confusion.

Two and a half days later I received a phone call that brought some clarity. Reshma and I have some dear friends in Spokane, Washington, Chip and Jerry Foster, who had a Bible college at that time where I had taught a few times. "Bruce," Chip said. "I had a dream last night."

I thought, *That's nice.*

"You were in it."

"Oh, really?" I'm thinking, maybe it was a nightmare.

"Yeah, you were teaching at the school and it was really interesting."

And....? I thought.

"You were teaching a subject I've never even heard of before."

"Well, what was that?"

"Translation by faith."

"What? Tell me about this!"

"There were only 12 students …"

"Good number."

"… you taught up to the 10:30 break and then said, 'If you want to understand and know the rest of this, follow me,' and you vanished and three of the students vanished with you.'"

Chip had my undivided attention.

"Do you remember the scriptures I was teaching on?" I asked.

She hesitated for a minute and then said, "Yeah."

"Write them down quickly please, I need them," I told her. She documented the scriptures from the dream for me.

When I had least expected it, a supernatural activation had taken place in my life. Though I was unsure of where to start, God had given Chip a dream that provided the scriptures on what would begin building the foundation. This experience left me undone and blown away!

And so, the adventure began. A couple of days later while sitting at my friend's house, I wanted to go by their pool to pray. Sitting by the pool, I began to pray and look at the Scriptures Chip had given me. Some, like Proverbs 2, were relevant to understanding and wisdom. Some were about gates, doors, windows, pathways, and double doors. All had a natural application and a supernatural application. This was my starting point as I began to study these revelations.

Sitting by the pool studying, I still felt overwhelmed and confused. "Lord," I said. "Why are You teaching me this? Never, ever in my whole life, or in my studies have I heard anybody talk about this subject."

The Lord answered, "You are a forerunner."

Oh, no! I thought. Have you ever studied church history about forerunners? It's not a pretty picture. It's like running through a minefield, and if you don't blow up, then everybody else gets to come through. That's a forerunner.

ENOCH

He said, "I'm raising you up to be a forerunner to teach My people how to do this by faith because the hour is coming when this will be the only way My people will be able to move around the earth."

I dropped and began to pray and worship God as it was frightening to me. Darkness is coming upon the earth and gross darkness upon the people, which is already here. Perverseness is already seen throughout the earth, and persecution of the Church is increasingly intense. We seem to have a breather right now, but it's going to become even darker after this brief lull. God is giving us mercy and grace to which we can prepare our hearts for walking in translation by faith.

After this encounter, I read the Bible more diligently, from Genesis to Revelation, the only way I know how to study. I didn't look up words in the Concordance; I read through the Bible. I found in the first book of Genesis that Adam and Eve enjoyed this type of interaction with God.

Enoch did too! Genesis 5:24 says, "Enoch walked with God, and he was not, for God took him." Remember the challenge to me was, "Do this by faith." I looked at that passage saying, "God, that was a sovereign act ... You did that, Enoch didn't exercise his faith."

"Keep studying," He said. I refuse to go to the Concordance or Thesaurus because we have access to a treasury of Scripture knowledge to find our course. From Genesis to Revelation was an unfolding in that manner. Hebrews 11:5 talks about Enoch again: "By faith Enoch was translated that he should not see death; and was not found, because God had translated him: for before his translation he had this testimony, that he pleased God (KJV)."

In 18 instances Enoch was quoted in the Word of God. 18 times he is either alluded to or quoted. Some of the earliest manuscripts of the Bible included the book of Enoch in the canon of Scripture but removed it because it was inconvenient for some as they didn't like the mysticism surrounding Enoch. The Ethiopian Bible still includes the book of Enoch. One of the most accurate books of Enoch is the Ethiopian book of Enoch. It's a good read! I'm not going to preach from it, but it's fascinating and provides more clarity and insight. Jesus, Paul and James considered it Scripture but we'll stick with the Bible God has given us for today.

Hebrews 11:5 says, "By faith, Enoch was translated." By whose faith? By God's faith? Think about that! Enoch made a decision to exercise his faith, and his faith said, "Lord, I don't want to die a natural death. I've seen eternity. By faith, I'm just going to come home." And that's what he did! Enoch walked with God for 300 years and didn't even "start" until he was 65 years of age. There's no excuse for us then, is there?

If you look at the Hebrew letters with a numeric equivalency, you'll find that 300 means "live long and prosper." Let me define that more: By faith, Enoch was transported and changed sides.

Transported can also allude to a means of conveyance, like a chariot of fire. Have you ever ridden in a chariot of fire? You can have all of the fancy cars in the world, but I like my chariot. You have a chariot too, and it fits nicely in your new heavenly mansion. Enoch was transported and changed sides so that he should not see death. Understand this, Genesis chapter 5 is under the lesser covenant which is a fallen system.

The Hebrew translation would read, "And Enoch walked with Aleph tav, God." "Aleph" is the first letter in the Hebrew alphabet and means "the first strong leader." That's God: number one Tav. The last letter was a cross, so this can be accurately translated by saying, "And Enoch walked in intimacy with the first strong leader who came in the sign of the Cross." That's the Word of God! He walked in intimacy with the Word of God or the God of the Word. That's why he had trust, so he could change sides.

Faith really means trust. You develop trust when you spend time with somebody. The alternative is that we strive to work up a carnal faith, but that'll get us nowhere. It doesn't work. As you develop a relationship, you come to know someone, and then trust begins to grow.

Enoch walked in a relationship with God, his trust and faith increasing daily. He enjoyed that intimacy with God—He could be relied upon, had unimpeachable character, His Word was true, and he could trust Him with his life. That's the key: The more you spend time with God, the more you trust Him and establish your faith in Him.

In the renewed covenant in which we walk, we have the blood of Jesus! Enoch gleaned revelation from his walk with God, but we glean Kingdom rights from the blood of Christ. You still must develop a relationship with God to learn how to exercise faith and walk with Him. You do that by spending time with the Lord. You can't come on the coat tails or the shirt sleeves of anybody else. You must establish this relationship for yourself.

Though the five-fold ministry of pastors, teachers, evangelists, prophets, and apostles are gifts to the body of Christ, they can only do so much in your life. You must pick up your own cross and follow Jesus. Don't come crying about this at the end of the age as you have a personal responsibility to walk with God. When we stop relying on others, we can start focusing on God. We're called to equip the church for the work of the ministry. God's work of ministry in this hour is spectacularly supernatural.

The more you spend time with God, the more you trust Him and establish your faith in Him.

Testimony of Translation

Last year, I was ministering in Germany at a Russian-German church. A brother approached me after I spoke briefly on this subject and said, "Finally! There's somebody I can share this with!"

"What do you have to share?" I asked.

"Two years ago, I came home from work at about 10 minutes to six o'clock," he said. "I wanted to attend a gospel meeting, but it was five hours away. Even though the meeting started at six o'clock, something in me compelled me to go. I told my wife, 'I've got to go to the meeting.' She said, 'You'll get there long after it's over. You can't go.' He said, 'I know that's true, but I have to go.' She said, 'Fine, go ahead and waste your time if you want.' By this time, it was five minutes to six. The man got in his car and pulled out of the driveway and four minutes later he called his wife. 'I'm there,' he told her. She said, 'You are not. You just left!' He said, 'No, I really am here. Remember my friend that was going also? He's right here with me.'"

This man told me, "I couldn't tell anybody that story because they'd think I'm nuts, but now I've met you, so I could tell you."

Many more Christians have had these extraordinary experiences but haven't talked about it because they don't want to be ostracized. It's sad that the Church would ostracize people that walk in the supernatural and don't want to accept anything outside of their purview or paradigm. Yet, it's also sad that he didn't have enough confidence in Christ and boldness to speak truth. That's a two-sided, double-edged sword. I understand why he didn't share, as many people don't want to accept that which God is doing.

You Are Not Alone in This

We were at the Eagles Nest Church with Garry Greenwald in California recently. When I was in Bible College, Garry had just started his ministry, and I was helping him with the lighting because my degree was in television broadcasting. The Lord had told me, "One day, you're going to speak at his pulpit for him."

I told the Lord, "Okay." About 11 years ago, we received a call with an invitation to come to their church. The guys inviting us said, "Pastor Garry said we could invite you, so we did, and we want you to teach on Translation by Faith."

I said, "Oh, I don't know about that!"

"No, go ahead," they said.

After praying about it, the Lord directed me to teach on translation by faith as they had requested. I suspected that I'd end up preaching there only once. I started teaching on translation by faith. Garry sat in the front row looking at me. When the message was over, I knew he was going to grab the mic and do the "Phil Donahue" interview thing. He asked me if he could ask me some questions and I agreed.

Turning to the people at the church he said, "This is a very strange message. How many of you have ever had a translation experience?" Five or six hands went up, so he called on them.

An elderly woman about 86-87 years old came up to the mic to share her story. "Some years ago," she said, "I was at home praying when all of a sudden, I was transported to England, taken to a hospital and into a hospital room where a woman was dying. Because she was on her deathbed, the Lord had me witness and minister to her. After she was instantly healed, I was translated back home."

I don't recall all of her story now but that story, along with her picture, was printed in a newspaper in England. Garry was quite astonished and asked her, "Why didn't you ever tell me that?"

Everywhere we've been, we find "closet transporters." It's time for us to shout it from the rooftops. Those desiring to be used of God in this way are going to take the dream and make it a reality. When you sing that old song, "I'll fly away," it's going to take on a whole new meaning!

The Measure of Faith

By faith Enoch was transported and changed sides so he shouldn't see death. He wasn't found because God had transported him, for before his transferal, he had this testimony that he was pleasing to God. The Lord arrested me there in my studies. "Read that again," He said. After I read it again, He said, "Read it again." And I read it again. The Lord had me re-read it four or five times. He said, "Read it again."

I said, "Okay Lord. What?"

"Did you notice what the key is?" He asked.

"Faith?"

"No. He was pleasing to Me. That's why his faith worked."

"Okay, how do you get to that level of pleasing You?"

"Haven't you read My Word? Without faith, it is impossible to please Me. Did I not tell you, when you were born again, I gave you a measure of faith? My people already please Me."

This takes it out of the realm of our works into the realm of His grace. You're already pleasing to God when you're born again. No buts! You're already pleasing to God. Nothing you could ever do will separate you from His love. However, if you want to be well pleasing to God, Hebrews 11:6 says, "But without faith it is impossible to please him: for he that cometh to God must believe that he is, and that he is a rewarder of them that diligently seek him" (KJV).

Therefore, faith without works is dead. Use your faith if you want to be well pleasing to God. As you seek to engage the Kingdom, do something by faith. I love the testimonies I've heard of the young people in different parts of the world as they're already highly engaged. In the spirit, they're walking around and circumnavigating bodies in the room because they're in a different dimension. It's phenomenal! That's faith in action. Sometimes people get sidetracked because of missteps or mistakes. "I tried that once and tripped over someone." Get up and go again! Do something by faith! Faith is always in action; it's never sedentary.

One man in the church I used to pastor put the word FAITH on the back of his chair. He'd say, "I've got faith!" Then he'd turn his chair around to show the word FAITH. It was a joke between us making a point that faith without works is dead. Most of the Church sits on their "blessed assurance" doing nothing and call it faith. We've got to be doers of the Word!

Acts of Faith

Reshma and I do little acts of faith wherever we go because we know it pleases God but also because it's an adventure.

We experienced one adventure in a coffee shop in Australia when I saw a little donation bin. I asked, "What's this?"

The server said, "Well, people donate so that those who come in and can't afford a coffee can have one for free. Usually, it's the elderly or street people because normally they can't afford a cup of coffee."

That's nice, I thought, and we sat down. "Let's put some money in," I said to Reshma.

Use your faith if you want to be well pleasing to God. As you seek to engage the Kingdom, do something by faith.

"What?" the server said. "Do you really want to do that?"

"Of course!" I answered.

Some people in our church worked in restaurants back in the day. I once said to one of them, "Sunday is when people in the church go out for breakfast and meals, so you must make good tips on a Sunday."

The woman I was speaking to said, "No! It's the worst day of the week."

"What do you mean?" I asked.

"The Christians are the stingiest people we've ever known!" she said. "They leave a mess on the table, they're demanding, and they never leave a tip."

"Oh, my goodness," I said. "You're kidding me!" Because this troubled me, I started taking young people from the church to the restaurant for a cup of coffee which was only about 50 cents back then.

When we were finished, I'd say, "Don't forget to tip." When they'd place a quarter on the table, I'd say, "That's not a tip. That's a statement of your inability to believe God!"

"What do you mean?" they'd ask.

They watched me put a 20-dollar bill on the table. "That's a tip!" I'd say. This wasn't about me; it was about helping them understand a biblical principle.

These young people became great tippers. It's amazing that when you tip somebody well, they'll wait on you hand and foot, treating you like royalty. They learned a key lesson: It's more blessed to give than to receive, and when you bless, you get blessed.

My mother followed this principle in Poland when she joined my dad, sister, and brother as tourists on a "Secret Service" underground church trip in the '80s. The hotel maids earned about a dollar per week. Mom would leave a little note with five dollars for the maid. They never ran out of soap or towels and received the best service while everyone else was running out of everything. Treat people the way you want to be treated. That's a Kingdom principle!

Invest yourself in character development. If you invest yourself in the Kingdom, God will invest in you. Though it's already yours, we all go through a process of growing up, so the more you invest, the quicker you'll grow! I wish I had learned that lesson long ago.

First in the Spirit

Did you know that you've already been translated? It happened the day you were born again. Colossians 1:13 says, "He delivered you from the powers of darkness and transferred you into the kingdom of the Son of His love" (KJV).

You've already had a translation experience and didn't know it, did you? People say, "But I'm physically here." Here's the mistake I made the first four or five years of my journey as the Lord walked this out with me. I equated the translation by faith of Enoch and Philip as physical. No! It's your spirit first. The physical is simply a garment called flesh. You're spirit first.

The Lord told me, "It's going to come in two phases. As you teach this, you're going to see it unfold in this way: First, people will be caught away in the spirit and then the physical translocations will take place." Three years ago, He said, "It's time for the second phase."

In June of 2014, I thought, *Wow! This is awesome Lord! I think I'm ready for my first lesson.* In the new year, we were doing a conference called Rending the Heavens. The pastor, a good friend, asked me "So, what is God talking to you about?"

Because he was a good friend, I said, "Well, translation by faith and you know …"

"Oh, you've got to start a school," he laughed. "You know, Translation 101."

"Yeah," I said, and we joked about it. "I'm not ready for that yet," I told him. "I've got a lot to study, a lot of revelation I still need."

Before worship started, he got up and said, "We'll be having an interesting time tonight because Bruce is going to teach on translation by faith."

No! I screamed inside. No!

The Lord said, "Just be quiet." During the worship, I had a difficult time entering into worship. I tried to be engaged but I was frantic, thinking, *What am I going to say?*

In Two Places at Once

Then, boom! I was caught away above the earth, and over Latvia. I asked the Lord, "Where are we?" I knew I was far up in the atmosphere; it was a cold winter night with a couple of cumulous clouds in the sky, and everything below was lit up. It reminded me of those photos from NASA space shoots where you see earth lit up with lights. I started descending through the clouds, even feeling the moisture as I passed through them.

You may wonder, Were you physically there? Whether in the body, out of the body, I don't know. It's irrelevant, but it was real. I entered into the top of a building going through the roof, then stood on the second floor in front of the door number 212. This is a fascinating prophetic number in Scripture and I encourage you to study it!

Next, I heard a little girl weeping. Her heart-rending sound of brokenness immediately moved me with compassion. Without asking the Lord, I opened the door and walked into a very small apartment flat. I didn't see anyone there but could hear weeping from behind another door. Walking through the door, I found a little eight-year-old girl, kneeling by the bed weeping, praying and crying out to God. As I knelt next to her, I knew that her name was Natalia, a good Russian name.

"Honey," I said. "What's the matter?" I had never studied the Russian language, yet Natalia understood me, and I understood her.

"Mommy and Daddy can't find work," she said. "We have not any food for a week and they're evicting us tomorrow." I prayed with her, comforted her, and then boom! I was back in the church again, still preaching.

A picture was taken of me during this encounter, and in the picture I'm literally transparent. You can find that picture on our website (stillwatersinternationalministries.org). At the time, I didn't equate this experience with translation because I wasn't that far along in my study to really understand it. I'd had my first lesson in translation and didn't even know it!

Later in June, I said, "Lord, I'm ready for my first lesson." I never understood why I heard Him chuckle until later when He gave me the answer: "You've already had the first lesson!"

More Lessons in Translation

My next lesson in translation was while driving from Seattle to Spokane, Washington, a distance of about 350 miles. I drove with a friend who had an old '77 beat-up car. Though I can't recall the make of his car, I knew that if we both pedaled fast enough, we could possibly get close to the speed limit. Chewing gum and barbwire held it together, and it was a mess. My friend used this car in his roofing business so between the smell and the possibility of sitting in roofing tar, it wasn't an ideal vehicle in which to ride.

As we started it up, I told him that the Lord had been teaching me about translation by faith. We prayed in agreement as I put my hand on the dash and said, "Father, I'm ready for my first lesson. Translate us!" As we started out, we played the worship CD, "This is the Air I Breath," singing in worship as we drove along.

At about the halfway point of the trip, we stopped to fill up with gas, rest, and eat lunch, which took about an hour. After our stop, we got back in the car and arrived at our destination in less than 90 minutes from when we left. A 5½-6-hour trip took us only 90 minutes.

"Lord," I said. "We were believing You for translation but what was that?" At the time I was a bit upset because I was trusting God and exercising my faith.

The Lord said, "That was your lesson."

That wasn't fair. "What was that?" I asked again.

He said, "You learn in school that the shortest distance between two points is what? A straight line?" And then He folded the line and said, "Unless you're God."

Science Finally Catching Up

I started studying physics though it wasn't my favorite subject and doesn't seem to work with my brain cells. New words and concepts in physics like "worm hole" or "wrinkle in time" left me a bit confused. I said, "Lord, how can this be?"

He said, "When you translate, you are stepping out of the realm of the natural—the realm of time—into the realm of the supernatural or eternity, where there is no time."

That explanation didn't help at all. I said, "Lord, I don't want the physics of this. I just want to walk in it." He got quiet, so I continued to study. Going forward, the Lord will also unpack this revelation for you, so keep going.

A Declaration

I believe, and make this declaration, that those who desire these revelations are going to experience it with God.

This will be a first lesson for some and an extended lesson with new revelation for others. It's time for this revelation and we're excited to see the manifestation of this reality. This generation has a destiny. Let me define a biblical generation: If you're alive, you're part of this generation. Though we've got to raise up the younger generation, we're all part of one generation. The younger generation is not going to surpass us, but we're going to do it together. I will not be left behind as I'm going with you. But we must reach the finish line together because this is the end of the age.

With gravity and humility, I know the Lord has given me an anointing and commission for translation by faith. As you read and receive this declaration and prayer, I believe the Lord is going to release that which you need in this hour. This isn't a prayer of hope, but a prayer of faith and bold declaration. It's up to you to carry this impartation with you and steward it. If you practice and utilize the tools you're given, you'll walk in the fullness of this revelation on translation. The key is passion. The key is passion. The key is passion.

Chapter Four

THE POWER OF THE SANCTIFIED IMAGINATION

A brother spoke to me not long ago, and said, "Where in the Bible does it say that you have the right, or that you're supposed to teach on this subject?" Then he went on to give me his arguments.

Quietly, I said to the Lord, "Lord, I need a good scripture for this." All Scripture is given by God and is profitable for reproof, correction and instruction. All Scripture, not just your favorite scripture.

Colossians 3:1 says, "If you have been raised up with Messiah, keep seeking the things above where Messiah is sitting at the right hand of God." You have permission to seek things above. You're commanded to do it and don't need any other permission. Verse 2 goes on to say, "Yes, feast on all the treasures of the heavenly realm and fill your thoughts with heavenly realities, and not with the distractions of the natural realm" (Colossians 3:2).

There's your permission! We should be pursuing the Lord with all that's within us, which includes the intellect but makes the intellect the secondary thing. We've allowed our intellect to obscure the things of the Spirit of God. We've got to put that in second place, being led of the Spirit, not by the intellect.

It's not difficult to experience a supernatural encounter with God. Didn't He say, "I will never leave you"? He's with you everywhere at all times, so it's not difficult to engage and walk into that realm. It becomes a tremendous adventure when you realize that you can walk in the supernatural and minister in ways that you've never dreamed of.

While teaching on this subject in Taiwan, I had a tremendous translator for the course of our time there. Sometimes when I speak, I get interpreters that are spot on because they flow with me, going back and forth with ease. On the second day of the meetings, she suddenly started stumbling.

I thought, *Perhaps I said something that she didn't understand.* I slowed down a bit in what I was saying and changed some words, but to no avail. For the next 10 minutes or so, she kept missing it until suddenly, it was perfect again. My thought at the time was that we were encountering spiritual warfare.

After the service, I asked, "What happened?"

"Oh Pastor," she said. "You don't understand."

"No, I don't," I said.

"While you were teaching," she explained, "I was caught away in the spirit and went to a beach in Japan. A little old lady was trying to carry a bucket of water back up to her home so I ran over to her and picked up the bucket. The only thing I had remembered of what you taught was that translating isn't for our own sake, it's for the sake of the gospel. So, I began to share the gospel with her,

THE POWER OF THE SANCTIFIED IMAGINATION

It's not difficult to experience a supernatural encounter with God. Didn't He say, "I will never leave you"?

and led her to Jesus. After that I was taken to the Middle East, but I've forgotten that encounter. Then, I came back here, and was with you again."

I said, "Well, in that case, it's okay!" Moving in the power of God like this makes ministry an adventure. I've told you about the realm of expectation and that if you stay in a place of expectation, God has permission at any time to interrupt your life. It gets to be fun! Sometimes it's amusing, sometimes it's frightening, but it's always fulfilling!

The Lord is looking for a people who are willing to lay down their agenda and embrace the "now" Word of God. You're a "now" people. Things are happening in the spirit. Those who've learned to engage in the spirit, pay attention to what God is doing!

Ephesians 1:15 says, "For this reason, because I have heard of your faith in the Lord Jesus and your love toward all the saints, I do not cease to give thanks to you, remembering you in my prayers." Didn't Paul say, "I pray in tongues more than all of you?" Here's an example of the Apostle Paul interceding for you. These prayers, because they've been written in Scripture, are ever and continuously being spoken. This is an eternal life-giving prayer for you right now.

Paul's words become a door, a portal or access point for you to begin to walk in the realm of the spirit. He said, "I'm praying that the God of our Lord Jesus Christ, the Father of glory, may give you the spirit of wisdom and revelation in the knowledge of Him. Having the eyes of your heart enlightened, that you may know what is the hope that He has called you to, and what are the riches of His glory and inheritance of the saints" (Ephesians 1:17-18).

Without belaboring this, if you study this passage of Scripture in the original language, you'll see what he's saying: "My prayer is that the Lord will give you wisdom so that you'll understand how to engage in the realm of the spirit through your sanctified imagination, so you might know your destiny."

The bridge between this realm and the supernatural realm is a sanctified, set apart, and yielded imagination that you give to God. The majority of Christians haven't learned to discipline their thought life and don't realize that it's the most powerful thing God has given them. Your ability to imagine and think when sanctified and yielded to God unlocks the door into the realm of the supernatural.

Our Father created everything first conceiving it in His imagination and then, as He meditated on it, it dropped from His imagination into His heart and out of the abundance of His heart, He spoke, "Let there be …" and it came into existence. That imagination became the bridge between the supernatural and the natural.

Though this is a powerful tool, we've been constantly, deliberately warned, "Don't consider the imagination because it's New Age." No! The imagination is as old as creation and belongs to the believer, not to the devil. The devil doesn't create anything, he only warps and twists truth. Much of what belonged to the Church was stolen by the devil who keeps it for his own use, trying to convince you that it's not yours.

That's demonic! Its imagination and the power have been stolen by the devil. I say, "Give it back!" If we go back to Scripture and apply the light of the truth of the Spirit of God, we learn that much of what the devil does has been established in Scripture but was stolen by the devil. The Church was then manipulated through propaganda and religious spirits to say, "These things are not God, that's the devil." Go back to the foundation of Scripture and you'll see the truth. It's quite simple.

Ezekiel 8:3 says,

"God grabbed Ezekiel by the lock of his hair and pulled him on the top of his head and he went into the spirit. And he put forth the form of a hand and took me by a lock of my head and the spirit lifted me up between the earth and the heaven and brought me in the visions of God to Jerusalem, to the door of the inner gate that looketh toward the north; where was the seat of the image of jealousy, which provoketh to jealousy" (KJV).

Ezekiel entered into the spiritual realm and saw some things. New Agers call that "astral projection." It becomes demonic because they warp and twist it. Then the Church gasps, and says, 'That's the devil!" No! That's the book of Ezekiel! We should be saying, "Devil, you can't have that! Give it back. That belongs to us!"

Several years ago, a 17-year-old boy was experiencing supernatural things where he'd be taken in the spirit. Literally taken into the Kremlin in Russia, he sat in on a Top-Secret council meeting and heard the plans they were making to do certain things to the earth. He was also taken into government meetings in China and with the American government. He had a wealth of knowledge, insight and revelation from actually being there in the spirit. When he tried to share what had happened with pastors and believers, they all said, "That's not God, that's the devil." After a while, he thought he was losing his mind.

Hearing his story, I said, "Young man, that's not the devil, that's God! It's a gift!" then showed him the proof in the Word. "Where you missed the mark," I told him, "was thinking you could share this experience with just anybody as you can't share it with just anybody. You must ask the Lord what you're supposed to do with these insights."

We have incredible precedence in translation by faith, like Elijah and Elisha. Throughout history, God's prophets have walked in this. The enemy would say, "Who keeps thwarting our plans to invade Israel?" They'd learn that the prophet was sneaking into their bedroom by the spirit at night. Even Paul said, "My spirit will go with you."

Some may think, "Oh, that's just a nice phrase" or "Oh, it says my heart is with you." No, Paul was there. Some are far more advanced in their ability to walk in the realities of translation by faith. If you have a passion to pursue this, the Lord will do something, so look for it! You're going to see something.

A Friendship with Jesus

God is saying, "I want you to sanctify your imagination and build a bridge." Many have heard of Neville Johnson and if not, look up his teachings, as you'll be greatly blessed. He's become a good friend of ours and has influenced my life tremendously.

Quite a few years ago, a man that Brother Neville knew by the name of Walter Buetler taught Neville how to see in the spirit in the early '70s. He taught Neville, "The bridge between the natural realm and the spirit realm is the bridge of a sanctified imagination."

Walter was a Bible schoolteacher and a pastor-missionary. He was a busy man, writing, teaching, and traveling. One day the Lord spoke to his heart. "Would you spend time with Me as a friend?" the Lord asked. "I don't have anybody that would just be My friend. Everybody comes to Me with petitions, requests and complaints, but nobody wants to be with Me and be a friend."

Of course, this request from the Lord Jesus moved his heart. Walter said, "Yes, Lord, I'll do that!" However, after making that commitment, he realized he didn't have time available. Knowing that he'd break God's heart if he didn't meet with the Lord as promised, he set aside 2:00 to 3:00 am to spend with the Lord as a friend. He set his alarm to get up at 1:50 am every night, washed his face, made a cup of tea, and then sat down in his easy chair.

Walter didn't know exactly what he was doing at that time, but would picture Jesus sitting in the empty chair across from him. Talking to Him as a friend, he'd say, "Lord, how was Your day? What do You think of this headline? How about the Yankees?" He hung out with Jesus like a friend.

Here's a key I want you to see: You can't develop a friendship if only one person is talking. Though I say this with love, we need to learn to shut up. When you communicate with God, be quiet and listen to His response. This type of interaction can be difficult in our instant society, as we want everything NOW.

Do you get offended when you speak to someone and they seem to ignore you or don't answer right away? With growing impatience, we might say, "Well ... are you going answer?"

If God equates a day to a thousand years and a thousand years to a day, and He says, "Wait a second," you might be sitting

The bridge between the natural realm and the spirit realm is the bridge of a sanctified imagination.

there for a week or two. Get used to that, but don't be troubled by it.

Walter Buetler began to communicate with God. He asked Him questions and then sat and waited for answers. Though it took some time, the Lord began to speak and communicate with him. The lag time between question and answer got shorter and shorter because he was developing focus, passion and an ability to hear with greater clarity. Every night, he spent that hour with the Lord, focused and saw Jesus. Because he imagined Jesus sitting with him, this time alone with God soon became his favorite time of the day.

One night, after one year of doing this, Walter got his tea, sat down, and prepared for his time with God. He knew that the Lord is punctual, so he waited. Suddenly, he heard the backyard gate open and close. Thinking about how strange it was to hear his back door open and close, he heard footsteps walk down the hall toward him.

Jesus walked in and sat down in front of him! The Lord said to him, "Because you have put this principle of focusing your sanctified imagination into practice, you will connect with your focus, and when the connection takes place, activation will come and you will see Me openly every day from now on."

Walter had focused on seeing Jesus for a year with a sanctified imagination, and then activation came so he could see Jesus with his eyes wide open. From that day forward and for the rest of his life, Walter saw—with open eyes— Jesus every day, everywhere he went. Walter's experience changed Neville's life, and after hearing the story, it drastically changed my life too.

Inspired by Walter's experience, I said, "Finally, somebody's telling me how to do this!" I started practicing, as Walter had done.

THE POWER OF THE SANCTIFIED IMAGINATION

The Lord is gracious so I don't get upset if I miss a day as it took me many years to get to the state I'm in. Knowing that it takes a while to develop a habit, I practiced, and practiced, and practiced.

I began this learning process while I was in Fred and Candy Wiker's house one day. Fred, a good friend, had ministered with Larry Randall, Bob Jones, Paul Cain, Bobby Conner and others who would stay in his home at times. Fred told me that whenever they came to stay, they'd all sit in a certain chair because they said it was a "think place." They'd sit in the chair and instantly connect with God. Hearing this I said, "Really? Can I sit there? What do I do?"

"You just sit down and focus," he said. That really didn't help.

"Just sit and wait on God," he suggested. That didn't help either.

"Just press in," he said.

Colossians 3:2 says, "Set your affection on things above, not on things on the earth" (KJV). That verse was the key for me in understanding what Fred was saying. I sat down, closed my eyes, and focused on the Lord, setting my affections on Him and things above. That's pressing in! Set your affections, your thoughts, your will, your mind, your emotions, and your imagination continually on Him, the One you love. If your mind wanders, don't get discouraged! Just bring your mind back to the focus of your affection.

I sat and sat and waited and waited. And do you know what I saw? Absolutely nothing! But I remained. I encourage you to speak to the Lord as you focus on Him, saying, "Jesus, I love You, Oh Lord, I love You." This helps keep me focused. As I continued expressing my love to Him, suddenly the "grey" I had been seeing started getting lighter and lighter, as if I was seeing through bushes. About 40 minutes later, it suddenly seemed like I entered through the bushes, emerged from a jungle, and stepped into Paradise. Seeing the city of God, I jumped out of the chair and cried out!

My friend Fred laughed. "See?" he said.

Settling into the chair again, the Lord took me back to Paradise and within a couple of minutes, I again saw the city of God and began speaking to Him as He stood next to me. Jesus spoke to me, sharing things to come. Some might say that was a vision, a translation, or an encounter. Yes! All of the above!

I continued to practice focusing and framing a picture of Jesus. One day we were holding a conference in a town near Seattle, Washington when my dad was in the front of the auditorium ministering alongside me and my friend, Andre Ashby. Suddenly, I looked at the Bible and saw an amazing purple color off to the side. Seeing purple was in itself a miracle because I was born with slight color blindness. Seeing this vibrant living purple caught my attention and as I looked at it, there stood Jesus, about 6'2," wearing a purple mantle over His white robe.

Seeing as I've been trained, I thought, *Did Jesus Christ come into flesh?* I was going to test the spirit because that's what we do. Even if it looks like Jesus, we must test the spirits.

Before I could even frame the question, He extended His hands to reveal nail prints. As He turned to me, I saw His blue, depthless eyes which no words can describe.

Some say, "But I saw His eyes, and they were green!" Good. He's got green eyes too. He's God! Everything you've received when you have an encounter with God speaks. Blue speaks of the prophetic, the heavenly realms and of life; green speaks of life and transition.

As Jesus turned to me with His indescribable eyes, love, compassion, joy and every good thing washed over me and hit me like a wave. Overwhelmed and changed forever, since that day, I can see Jesus.

THE POWER OF THE SANCTIFIED IMAGINATION

As Jesus turned to me with His indescribable eyes, love, compassion, joy and every good thing washed over me and hit me like a wave. Overwhelmed and changed forever, since that day, I can see Jesus.

Effort, passion, and desire made this experience a reality. The tools I'm giving you took years for me to learn, but if you put these tools into practice from this day forward, you'll walk in this too.

In the book of Acts, Jesus led the disciples out to Bethany, where He ascended into heaven. As Jesus ascends, two angels stand there saying, "Which also said, Ye men of Galilee, why stand ye gazing up into heaven? This same Jesus, which is taken up from you into heaven, shall so come in like manner as ye have seen him go into heaven" (Acts 1:11, KJV).

I love that story because the disciples weren't impressed with the angels, they were overcome as they kept looking at Jesus. Their focus, passion and purpose were fixed on Christ, the same focus of angelic hosts. Many people today say, "Oh, I want to see angels!" No! You want to see Jesus! The angels accompany Him. The angels said, "In the same way He left, He comes again," so we have an eschatology that says He's going to return in the clouds. From Jesus' bodily resurrection morning until His ascension was a 40-day period of time in which He appeared to the majority of the Church.

In the same way He left, He's coming again! That's why He's speaking so loudly today as it's like a clarion call to the Church: Get ready! He's coming again because He's doing what He said

He would do. He's declaring the end from the beginning, the birth of the Church.

10 days later (one significant meaning of the number 10 is test), the disciples had to tarry. Hidden away as they were afraid of the Jews and didn't want to be killed, they tarried in Jerusalem until the Holy Ghost visited them as flames and tongues of fire came upon them. Emboldened by the Holy Spirit, they could never be moved from that conviction again.

Before Jesus went to the cross, He said, "I'm going to go and be crucified."

Peter stood up and said, "Lord, I will never leave you, even if the others do!" Before the resurrection, Peter only had an intellectual understanding of Jesus. But, after the resurrection and being endued with power from on high, Peter's intellectual understanding became a heart understanding. He said, "I'm not going to deny Jesus again." When Peter knew he was going to be crucified, he said, "Crucify me upside down because I'm not worthy to be crucified in the same manner as my Lord."

From Practice to Lifestyle

We must move from the mind to the heart and from practice to lifestyle. We must start somewhere and build into reality. The sanctified imagination is the bridge that will take us there.

Some time ago, I was teaching in a small California town in the isolated Mojave Desert. Other than the highway, there was nothing there but tumbleweeds and a few people. During worship at the church, I had a vision. I've learned to close my eyes during these times, as it's the ideal time to connect with God. With eyes closed I said, "Lord, what are You saying to these people?"

As I asked this question of the Lord, I saw a meteorite. Thinking my imagination was making something up, I said, "Eyes, stop that! That's only my imagination."

Closing my eyes again, I repeated, "Lord, what are You saying?" I saw the meteorite again.

As this continued, I became frustrated. "Lord, I'm trying to cast down these imaginations, but I'm having a difficult time," I told the Lord.

Another meteorite appeared. Then the Lord spoke to me, "Prophesy!"

"What?" I said. God was showing me a picture of that meteorite as a prophetic sign for those people. And it came to pass!

Where was that meteor? Where was I seeing that meteor? In my imagination! Because God speaks through the imagination, many people don't recognize His voice and don't recognize the activations taking place because they reason to themselves, thinking, "Well, that's just me." Sorry, but you're not that brilliant or creative. It's better to err on the side of faith than on the side of doubt. Move toward God, not away from God. He will bring course correction when necessary. If you trust Him, you'll never be disappointed.

The Lord wants to open the eyes of our imagination so we can properly frame the pictures of the Kingdom. Ephesians 1:18 says, "I pray that the light of God will illuminate the eyes of your imagination, flooding you with light, until you experience the full revelation of the hope of his calling—that is, the wealth of God's glorious inheritances that he finds in us, his holy ones!" (KJV).

This is a scriptural confirmation of that which we focus on, we connect with, and that which we connect with brings activation. Sometimes, God does this sovereignly and sometimes He makes us work a bit for it. He's always involved though because He's trying to lead and guide us into Christlikeness.

It's all about the Kingdom; it's not about us. Taking ourselves out of the equation enables us to move forward. Putting ourselves in the equation trips us up. God wants to enlighten our eyes so we'll know the immeasurable greatness of His power toward us who believe, according to the working of His great might that's in us.

Ephesians 1:19-20 says,

"And what is the exceeding greatness of His power to us who believe, according to the working of his mighty power that was released when God raised Christ from the dead and exalted him to the place of highest honor and supreme authority in the heavenly realm" (KJV).

He worked in Christ when He raised Him from the dead and seated Him at His right hand in heavenly places, far above—not a little bit above—all principality, and power, and might, and dominion, and every name, character and authority that's known in existence, not only in this world, but also in that which is to come (Ephesians 1:21, KJV). He's lifted above, not only in this age but in the age to come.

He put all things under His feet and gave Him as head over all things to the Church, which is His body, the fullness of Him who fills all in all. In this description, Jesus is The Overcomer, and having finished His work, He's been given power, authority, and dominion.

Ephesians 2:2-7 says,

"But God, being rich in mercy, because of the great love with which he loved us, even when we were dead in our trespasses, made us alive together with Christ—by grace you have been saved—and raised us up with him and seated us with him in the heavenly places in Christ Jesus, so that in the coming ages he might show the immeasurable riches of his grace in kindness toward us in Christ Jesus" (KJV).

Let's go back to Ephesians chapter one where Jesus is seated at the right hand of the Father. You are also seated with Him at the right hand of the Father, far above all rulers, all authority, and all dominion because you're in Christ.

You have authority over every name, character, authority or manifestation of power other than God. He put everything under His feet, and since you are the body of Christ and the lowest point of the body is the feet, it's all under your feet. God appointed Jesus to be head over all things to the church.

The implications of this are beyond comprehension and require the Spirit of God to enlighten us. We're already victorious and have seated ourselves. That means it's finished in Him, in the eternal realm where you live and move and have your being. It's not a stretch for us to engage and walk in the eternal realm naturally, seasonally or momentarily as we're already there.

Engage your physical and spiritual senses to engage what God wants you to do in both realms. You may wonder how you can engage your physical senses in the spiritual realm. If you've ever felt an anointing, then you've done it, as that's an engaging of physical senses in the spiritual manifestation. Have you ever felt the heat, the love, the joy? In those moments your spirit-man is taking the ascendant position and your physical body is following,

You have authority over every name, character, authority or manifestation of power other than God.

so you're tasting, touching, seeing, and smelling. Yet it doesn't stop there. You can also go there.

This is the norm for a believer. Believe! To walk in this, you've got to believe it's yours! It is yours! It doesn't just belong to a "special few," but is available to all believers. As it says in 1 John 4:17, "As He is, so also are we in this world" (KJV).

The Book of Mysteries

On Rosh Hashanah, 2017, I had an encounter with Jesus as the King of Glory (when He comes as the King of Glory). Falling flat on my face in worship, I was lost in His presence. When that glory (kabod) of God lifted, I was able to stand, yet my legs were unsteady beneath me, and I could barely function.

Enoch approached me carrying what looked like a large book similar to the giant family Bibles many have seen. "Sir," I said. "Why are you here?"

Handing me the book, he said with great authority, "This is the book of mysteries I began to write when I walked the earth. Now finish it."

He made this declaration to the Church—the body of Christ—not to an individual. He's telling us that we're going to finish the mysteries, fulfill those mysteries and walk in those mysteries in which he began to walk.

He then gave me his mantle, which means the mantle is released to you. Receive this mantle as it belongs to this generation. When I get glimpses into that book of mysteries, He leaves me undone. That book of mysteries contains revelation that baffles anything one could imagine.

For example, did you realize that as a believer, you can terraform the earth? Let me give you an example of terraform: As this revelation comes forth, as a believer and son of God, one seated with Christ, you can walk in the desert as Moses did and say, "Water, come forth! Life, come forth! Abundance, come forth!" and it will spring forth. The Lord is investing in this generation what is beyond anything we could think or dream. He's putting authority, power, and revelation in us. You'll find yourselves in situations where that authority, power and revelation will explode and spring forth out of you.

In 1 Kings 17 is Elijah, one of my favorite prophets in the Old Covenant. Elijah came out of obscurity, exploding onto the scene in 1 Kings chapter 17. Elijah proclaimed a drought and so likely wasn't a popular prophet. Prophets of old didn't care about popularity, unlike the prophets of today who need a daily fancy stroking-ego word to keep the money coming. No! Prophets like Elijah didn't care about the accolades of men, they cared about obedience to God.

In chapter 18, the Lord says, "Go present yourself to Ahab." Imagine that! Elijah is the most wanted man in Israel, Ahab wanted to kill him, yet the Lord tells Elijah to meet with him. You better be hearing from God when you get an instruction like that. In obedience, Elijah set out on his way.

> "Now it happened after many days that the word of the Lord came to Elijah in the third year, saying, "Go, show yourself to Ahab, and I will send rain on the face of the earth" (1 Kings 18:1, NASB).

In other words, confront dominions of Jezebel, and then I will release revival. Rain speaks of blessings, life and revival. If that's the case, then we don't want showers of blessings, we want a deluge! We've been witnessing unnatural disasters occurring all over the world, in particular, unusual levels of rainfall causing rivers to overflow and flood. The deluge we're seeing in the natural realm is a sign that God is about to pour out His Spirit in all the earth. Don't look at it as a negative disaster but consider it a promise of God! This is what the Spirit is saying because Scripture says the natural comes first, then the spiritual.

> "However, the spiritual is not first, but the natural; then the spiritual" (1 Corinthians 15:46, NASB).

If the Church learns to walk in translation by faith, when a natural disaster occurs, we'll go to the location to raise the dead, heal the sick and proclaim the Good News. When the task is fulfilled, we'll return home. God is raising up this generation so those people will know that God has been there.

The famine was severe in Samaria, so Ahab summoned Obadiah, the steward of the palace. As seen in 1 Kings 18:7, Obadiah feared God Adonai: "When Obadiah was on the road, all of a sudden, Elijah met him. Then Obadiah recognized him, he fell facedown and said, 'Is it you, my lord Elijah?'"

All of a sudden means out of nowhere. Note that when he recognized Elijah, he said, "Is that really you?" Befuddled, in awe and fear, he couldn't think logically or clearly. "Elijah said, 'It is I. Go tell your lord, 'Look Elijah is here.'"

Obadiah is terrified and says, "How have I sinned, that you are giving your servant into the hand of Ahab to put me to death?" Anyone who said, "I saw him" when Elijah wasn't there, had been put to death.

Pay close attention to his explanation: "It will come about when I leave you that the Spirit of the Lord will carry you where I do not know; so, when I come and tell Ahab and he cannot find you, he will kill me, although I, your servant, have feared the Lord from my youth" (1 Kings 18:12, NASB).

It's like saying, "Look, Elijah is here but as soon as I leave you, the Ruach Adonai may carry you off, where I wouldn't know." Historically, Elijah was considered one of the most mystical prophets because he would come and go, vanishing with no natural reason.

We need to be like the prophet Elijah as the Spirit of God carries us off or translates us. You are the Elijah generation just before the return of Messiah. Remember that Elijah left this world in a chariot of fire and didn't see death.

How about you? What are you saying and confessing? We can't confess these supernatural things of God into being, but we can confess it into our spirit in agreement with what God is saying into this generation.

A Prophetic Word

I spoke my first prophetic word at age four. I wasn't saved and hadn't even been to church. My dad, brought up in the Catholic Church, went on to Catholic seminary to become a priest but left that pursuit because it didn't fill the God-sized hole in his heart. Once he married and had kids, he was busy working with seven mouths to feed.

One day while playing in the living room of our house in Canada, I suddenly stopped and said, "it's going to be neat to be here when Jesus comes back."

My brother and sister stopped playing, looked at me and said, "Who's that?"

"I don't know," I said.

A week later, the devil tried to kill me. I was put in an oxygen tent after being misdiagnosed three times with pneumonia, which almost took my life. A year later, we were driving down the highway and I was playing with the door handle. There were no seatbelts back then, so the door flew open and I went flying out of the car. With supernatural assistance, I tucked and rolled, and suffered no injury whatsoever.

The enemy doesn't want me—or you—to fulfill our calling and destiny. If you're living and moving in the power of God, he knows who you are, and doesn't like you.

We ministered in an East Indian church in Portland where the pastor had great difficulty because of a mixture of attitudes within the congregation. Many were pantheistic in their "understanding" of God, believing that Jesus was just another one of them. After ministering there, a woman came up and said, "Thank you so much for coming. We really appreciate you coming."

"No, it's our pleasure," I said.

Suddenly a demonic voice spoke through her and said, "We know you! We've heard all about you!"

At first, I thought, *Oh, good. You're going to hear a lot more!* Knowing that the enemy had heard about me, excited me! I'm a threat to the enemy, and so are you!

As you walk in this revelation, you're a threat to the devil because every place you step into with this revelation, he must move out. Everything he thought was his is no longer his. The deception in the Church is no longer effective on you because you're walking in the powers of the age to come. We say, "The powers of the age to come" because the vast majority of believers won't engage in this until that age comes.

God always has a forerunner company of believers. Elijah, in his day, was translating. Enoch and Ezekiel were forerunners. Most of the Church is like the children of Israel when Moses ascended Mt. Sinai. Though invited, they say, "No, no! That scares us. You go and tell us what He says." Or, "No, if we go up there, we'll die."

I say, "What a way to go! In the face and presence of God!" He's calling a forerunner company of believers, and you're in that company.

The Chariots of Fire

Elijah not only translocated but he had a chariot of fire experience. When Reshma and I were ministering in John and Ruth Filler's church in Coeur d'Alene, Idaho many years ago, this revelation was new to us. John and Ruth had been gracious and said, "Be out of the box and do whatever God shows you to do."

"God, you'd better speak to me!" I prayed. Suddenly, I saw a chariot of fire come into the room. I glanced at it, then thought, *No, no, no ... I'm not going to say a word.*

The Lord said, "Tell them!"

"Lord," I prayed, "If I tell them, they'll never invite me back."

"If you don't tell them," the Lord said, "I'll never let you come back."

John and Ruth were seated at the platform and intercessors were stationed at the four corners of the auditorium. Turning to John and Ruth, I said, "Out of the box?"

"Yes," they said.

I said, "I see a chariot of fire." I don't know what was going on in their heads and didn't ask them what they thought that night. We moved on, and I thought, *Okay, good. All is well.*

The next night during the meeting the chariot came into the room again. "Oh no, Lord!" I prayed. "No. No. No!"

"Tell them," He said.

"Oh Lord, please!" I pleaded.

"Tell them," He said again.

Turning again to John and Ruth, I said, "Out of the box?"

"Yes, yes," they said. "Out of the box."

After I told them what I was seeing, the Lord said to me, "Put two chairs there in the front of the church."

I called the ushers, and said, "Ushers, put two chairs there."

"Now Lord, what next?" I prayed.

"Have John and Ruth come and sit there in the chairs," He said.

I asked them again, "Out of the box?"

"Yes," they said, so I instructed them to come.

"You guys come and sit here in the chairs."

John told me afterward that he was thinking, *What is this guy doing?* When they sat in those chairs (in the chariot) and we prayed, they were caught away in the spirit for an hour!

The next couple who sat in the chairs were also caught away for an hour. These chairs—the chariot—became a portal, a gateway, and an access point into the realm of the spirit.

The chairs still sit in the church to this day, only there are two chariots now. People continued to come and set up to 20 chairs out in the chariot. Scientists, pharmacists, and people trained in logical reasoning would sit there and say, "I've never had an experience like that."

Simple obedience to the instruction of God, showing up the foolishness of the mind, leads to powerful encounters. It doesn't matter if you look foolish as many already think you already look foolish. When you do what God says to do, it will often bypass your logical reasoning mind. Some may say, "Well, that's not decorous, you know. That's not dignified." Being willing to become

Being willing to become foolish in the eyes of the world and become wise in the eyes of God is where true wisdom lies.

foolish in the eyes of the world and become wise in the eyes of God is where true wisdom lies.

In addition to Ezekiel, Elijah and Enoch, Philip was physically caught away in the spirit:

> "When they came up out of the water, the Spirit of the Lord snatched Philip away and the eunuch no longer saw him but went on his way rejoicing. But Philip found himself at Azotus, and as he passed through, he kept preaching the gospel to all the cities until he came to Caesarea" (Acts 8:39-40, NASB).

I love that story! Philip was one of the first to have a revival in the church. Off he went to Samaria, the whole city filled with joy, being affected by the gospel. In the middle of the revival, the Lord said, "Leave."

Many people today would say, "Whoa, wait Lord! I've worked for this all my life. I haven't even finished printing the T-shirts! The CDs were just made. C'mon!"

Understanding authority and obedience, Philip calls the apostles and says, "Here, take it (the work/ministry). I have to go." After starting a huge revival, God tells him to go into the wilderness where there's nothing. Yet as Philip walked in the desert, he suddenly had an encounter with an angel, which he would have missed if he hadn't obeyed.

Further down the road Philip encounters the Ethiopian eunuch reading a book in a chariot. He may have thought, *Oh, so this is the one. You made me leave a thousand to come to the one?* Yes, God values each one!

After Philip helped the eunuch understand Scripture, he said, "Look! There's a mud puddle over there! What keeps me from being baptized?" Philip baptized him, and when they came up out of the water, Philip found himself physically 28 miles away!

Ruth Filler testified that as she stepped in the "chariot," God took her back in the spirit to witness Philip's encounter with the eunuch. Going back in time, she saw him translate. This excited me because it's in God's Word, and if it's in the Word, it's mine. All the promises of God are "Yes and Amen!"

I Have Set Before You an Open Door

I was in my office one day after reading about Philip's translation in Scripture. Praying and walking back and forth, I said, "Oh Lord Jesus, this is awesome, Lord! I'm ready for my next lesson!"

Suddenly, I found myself standing in the void of space, looking at the stars. Seeing this symphony of worship and praise overwhelmed me.

As I grew up, I dreamed of becoming a fighter pilot and astronaut. I made models, read books, learned instrument flight rules, visual flight rules and regulations, had posters in my room of various cockpits and could name every World War II aircraft and other aircraft built up to that point. I could even name every component of the Apollo Aircraft. I was passionate! After learning that because of my partial color blindness I couldn't get accepted into the training, my dream died.

THE POWER OF THE SANCTIFIED IMAGINATION

Now, standing in the stars, I thought, *Lord, send the Space Shuttle by, so I can tell them I made it! Maybe I can tag the shuttle 'Bruce was here.'* Looking at the vast expanse of the universe, I saw no planet earth. In awe, I had no fear as this was fun to me. Seeing the expanse and listening to the worship, I could only say, "Wow!"

Suddenly, I saw a flash of light. Looking toward the flash, I saw a door far out in the distance. The door opened to the right with light emanating from it. As I looked at the door, I heard the Lord say, "Go ahead."

As I took a step toward the door by faith, I stepped through the door and stepped into an empty office room that measured about 600 square feet. Out the window of the office, opposite the building, I saw a black marble façade building with tinted windows and a grey building next to it. I saw a detailed layout of the streets around the buildings.

It was early on a bright sunny morning and I knew in my spirit that I was in Sydney, Australia. I said, "Lord, I've always wanted to come here!"

In my excitement, I headed toward the door to explore the area, but before I got too far, the Lord said, "That's your lesson. Go back."

Looking around, I saw one door that led to the bathroom. So, by faith, I stepped through the doorway and was back in my room.

While in Australia last fall, we looked for the street I had visited. Coming back from the airport a different way than we had in the past because of traffic, I saw it! "That's it!" I said. "God is awesome!"

A friend named John used to be a worship leader at a well-known church. One morning, he received a phone call from a friend saying, "Thank you so much for coming to the hospital last night and praying for my wife. She's better now."

"What are you talking about?" John asked.

"John, you were here," his friend said.

"I'm in Seattle and you're in New York, I was not there, I was sleeping!"

His friend said, "No. You were here!"

"No, I wasn't."

"Yes, you were" he said, "We have a picture of you."

What an amazing testimony of what God is doing!

Let me warn you, however, to not look for evidence of translation encounters or take physical evidence of a spiritual act of God. God will provide evidence when necessary.

Some will run into people you ministered to in other parts of the world and when they recognize you, you'll say, "Wait, wait, when did that happen?

You might say, "That can't be, as I was at home." Then you'll realize that the dream you had was a genuine encounter. This is beginning to happen throughout the world.

I call one of my favorite experiences in God, "Jesus and mass transit." I'd like you to see a wonderful place in Paradise where you can drink from the river, an offspring of the River of Life, called the River of Revelation. When you drink from that river, you receive a download, then you eat the fruit from the tree. It's an amazing place!

John 6:16 says,

"When evening came, at the end of the age, his disciples went down to the sea or out to the nations, they got into the boat, and went over the sea to Capernaum, and it was already dark."

Why would it say evening came and it was already dark? The decline of light came at the setting of the sun, or the end of the age, and as you near the end of the age, it gets dark. We've witnessed this in our lifetime. It's going to get increasingly worse in the world, but the light will increase in the Kingdom.

Verse 17 says, "And Jesus had not come to them." I marvel at this. I came from an "almost-of-God" denomination where they did ministry without Jesus, following a program and formula.

In Bible college, in preaching class, we were expected to deliver three points before the closing of the message. I asked, "Can I just close and not do any points?" as I was terrified at that time. You couldn't pay me to stand up in front of people to talk. Thank God, He set me free of the fear of man.

While the disciples were on the water, John 16:18 says, "The sea arose." The sea speaks of the nations. "There was a great wind, upheaval, and it was blowing." We see upheaval and chaos throughout the nations now.

"So, when they had rowed ..." (v 19) speaks of their program. "It's a hard ministry. Man, I work hard in ministry," some ministers say. Well, stop it! Rest! They were half-way across the lake when they saw Jesus walking on the sea (walking across the nations). Millions of people are being saved throughout the earth today as Jesus appears to them. He's walking across the nations.

When they saw Him, they were terrified, as they thought it was a ghost. This was so far out and beyond any religious practice or experience, that they reasoned it couldn't be God.

In the same way, some say, "I don't know if I agree with that brother," which used to bother me. People would try to argue, saying, "God doesn't do that."

I prayed, "Lord, what do I say to these people?"

"Just agree with them," He said. So, when people tried to argue, I'd say, "You know what? I agree with you."

"You do?" they'd say with surprise.

"Yes," I'd tell them. "Be it done to you according to your faith. But as for me and my house, we walk in this …"

They're afraid, as the disciples were in the boat. Visitation is a scriptural principle. When the Lord said, "No, don't be afraid, it's Me," they received a revelation. Receiving the revelation, they invited Him into their boat (ministry), which brought activation. The moment Jesus stepped into the boat, they were immediately at the other shore. This opportunity to invite Him in is yours in this hour as He wants you to walk this walk with Him.

"Mama" Jenkins, who lived on earth for 106 years, was a good friend of Reshma and mine. Smith Wigglesworth prophesied her birth to her father and said, "I'm going to be her spiritual father and I will mentor her." This little old black woman from the south had a profound mantle and anointing and walked with Smith Wigglesworth until he went home to be with the Lord.

In the '50s, God supernaturally took Mama Jenkins to a hospital where the first operation was being performed to separate Siamese twins. She walked in and prayed over the twins before the complicated surgery. The nurses returned to the room in speechless shock. There lay the twins, separated successfully, before surgery took place!

Mama Jenkins lived a supernatural life. The Lord told her that she could remain here until the end if she'd like, but she saw what was coming and said, "It's too putrid and ugly; I don't want to be here." I was honored when Mama Jenkins called me her spiritual son. I don't know why she did, but I'll take it! My attitude is Yes! Impart that to me!

Four or five years ago while ministering in the U.S., Mama Jenkins came to our meeting. At 106, she was still driving! It was fun to watch her because people would ask, "How old are you? And you're still driving?"

She'd say, "Well, of course, I'm driving! What do you think I am? An invalid?"

When the meeting was over and we were leaving the meeting, we said, "We're going out to eat, Mama. Do you want to come?"

She said, "Okay." We walked out of the church together. There's only one way to get to the restaurant we had chosen. We left for the restaurant as Mama Jenkins walked slowly behind us. Yet, when we arrived at the restaurant, her car was already parked there and she was inside!

"How did you do that?" I asked.

Grinning, she said, "Oh, I got my ways." Mama Jenkins was one who walked in translation by faith.

Chapter Five

THE REALM OF EXPECTATION

"And behold, an angel of the Lord suddenly appeared and a light shone in the cell; and he struck Peter's side and woke him up, saying, 'Get up quickly.' And his chains fell off his hands. And the angel said to him, 'Gird yourself and put on your sandals.' And he did so. And he *said to him, 'Wrap your cloak around you and follow me.' And he went out and continued to follow, and he did not know that what was being done by the angel was real, but thought he was seeing a vision. When they had passed the first and second guard, they came to the iron gate that leads into the city, which opened for them by itself; and they went out and went along one street, and immediately the angel departed from him. When Peter came to himself, he said, 'Now I know for sure that the Lord has sent forth His angel and rescued me from the hand of Herod and from all that the Jewish people were expecting'" (Acts 12:7-11, NASB).

"Now behold! Look, an angel of the Lord." That's visitation! "An angel of the Lord stood by Peter and a light shone in the prison." That's the glory of God! Can you see the glory of God with the naked eye? Is it biblical? Remember the story of God leading the children of Israel with the pillar of fire by night and the pillar of cloud by day in the book of Exodus? Yes! You can see the glory of God! We should expect it.

Notice that the angel struck Peter on the side and raised him up saying, "Arise quickly!" This is living proof that sometimes God really needs to slap some sense into us to get our attention.

Recently, while we were ministering, a group of angels were crowding me and standing very close. I couldn't back up and kept bumping into them, so it wasn't long until I was almost off the platform. Like a moving wall behind me, they kept bumping me forward. I inquired of the Lord about this, but the Lord hasn't told me what that was all about.

The reality is that you can physically encounter beings from heaven—Elijah, Abraham, Amos, Joshua and many others experienced such encounters. The physical and supernatural interact on a regular basis and through that interaction, an element of translation or translocation takes place.

In this chapter of Acts, the angel told Peter, "Put on your sandals and your mantle and follow me," then the gates of the prison opened supernaturally and he walked out! Peter must have thought, *I must be dreaming!* Was this in the body or out of the body? He didn't know if it was real until the angel vanished and he found himself outside the prison.

Physical Manifestations of Walking in God's Glory

God is doing wondrous works in this hour. We know of a Native American apostle from Anchorage, Alaska whose wife had stage-four cancer. The medical people had done everything they could do for her. This couple kept praying, but as they prayed, they continued looking for an alternative method for a cure. In a last attempt to bring healing to her body, they drove down to an alternative clinic they had heard of located in Arizona near the Mexican border. After driving almost 4000 miles to the clinic, she underwent treatment, but it wasn't effective.

On the way back, they said, "Let's take our time, enjoy the trip and enjoy our time together." They went to Las Vegas, Nevada, where one of their daughters lived. Mom and Dad were at the hotel and their daughter came to stay with them. The daughter wasn't following the Lord and didn't believe all this "stuff" her parents believed.

One day the mother said to her daughter and husband, "Why don't you two go down to Walmart? It's only a couple of blocks away and you can buy some snacks and some water for us."

Encounters with Angels

After deciding to go, the father and daughter began to walk and talk, sharing and visiting together as they hadn't seen each other for a while. When they arrived at Walmart, a young lady was sitting in the rather large entryway, begging. Appearing to be about 25 years old, she was disheveled and dirty, wearing raggedy clothes. When the man and his daughter saw the girl, he looked at her with great compassion and approached her. Many watched as he walked up to her, reached in his pocket and handed her $500-$700. "Young lady, you don't have to live like this," he said. "You can buy some new clothes, get some food, and then rent a hotel room and clean yourself up." Then he prayed with her.

Leaving the girl, he turned to go into the store. As bystanders continued to watch the girl, he saw their eyes widen in shock.

When one woman screamed, he didn't turn around to look, but asked the woman, "What happened?"

"She vanished!" she replied.

"Oh!" he said, "That was an angel on assignment." After witnessing to the people in the Walmart entryway, he led them all to the Lord, and they rejoiced and worshiped God, dancing, singing and having a great time.

After this transpired, his daughter was weeping as she had witnessed tangible evidence of a supernatural God. As she wept, an African American brother said to her, "I'm a taxi driver so if you need a ride when you're done shopping, I'll be outside waiting for you. I'll give you a ride to wherever you're going."

"Okay," she said.

After they did their shopping and came out of the store, the daughter continued to weep. The taxi driver, who had been waiting as promised, pulled his car up, opened the door and said, "Let me take you." As he drove them, he rejoiced about all that had happened.

When they pulled up to the hotel and got out of the taxi, the daughter said to her father, "Don't forget to pay him." After reaching into his pocket, he turned around to find that the taxi and driver had vanished. I bet you didn't know they have taxis in heaven. They vanished! In awe of God, the girl began weeping again.

The next day after saying their goodbyes, hugging each other and praying together, Mom and Dad got in the car with a 4000-mile journey ahead of them. But as they pulled out of the hotel driveway in Arizona and turned left, they turned left into the driveway of their home in Anchorage, Alaska. Instantly transported home!

I asked the man later about this story. "Why didn't you turn around to see what had happened in that Walmart?"

THE REALM OF EXPECTATION

He laughed and said, "I just knew what had happened. The Lord had been speaking to me about angels on assignment appearing all over the earth and I just knew!"

"Brother," I said, "has that ever happened to you before?"

"Well, a few times," he replied.

"Do you think that's going to become more normal now-a-days?" I asked.

"Oh, absolutely!" he said.

"Do you want to sell your car?" I asked. "It gets good mileage!"

I'm revealing these things to you to build expectation in your heart. I want you to come to the place where before you go somewhere and before you get in your vehicle, you'll lay your hands on it and say, "Father, I thank You that translation is mine! Amen." Start exercising your faith because God responds to faith and expectation. Expect Him to take you to your destination.

Physical manifestations of supernatural encounters with angelic beings occurred in Peter's day and are happening today!

Reshma and I had an encounter some years ago while ministering in a small church in Pennsylvania. Out in the country, this church was very old and had no indoor plumbing. You'd have to go out back to the outhouse to use the restroom!

We had finished ministering and were leaving the church at about 8-8:30 pm when an old Ford pick-up truck pulled into the church parking lot. The guy driving said, "Is this where Brother Allen is ministering?"

Reshma said, "Oh, we just finished. So sorry."

"Hi, I'm Bruce," I said to the man.

"I just drove 85 miles to hear you speak tonight," he explained. As I shook his hand, I noticed that he had powerful hands like a construction worker.

"I'm so sorry," I said. "We'll be here tomorrow if you want to come back. But here, since you came this far, let me give you a copy of my book."

"Okay," he said. "Thank you."

As we turned around and started walking toward our car, we thought that since we were going out to eat, we ought to invite him to join us. But when we turned around, he—and his truck—were gone. The road was straight for miles and there was no way he could have driven away! He had vanished! Reshma and I felt convicted and said, "Oh! We should have asked him sooner!"

We've experienced many encounters like this where one minute, we're talking to somebody, then we turn for a moment and they're gone. LIVE IN EXPECTATION.

You must treat others with respect, especially if you don't know them. You never know to whom you're speaking.

Heaven is Invading Earth in this Hour

Heaven is invading earth and Christians are invading heaven in this hour. Something has shifted in the spiritual realm. We're now walking in a revelatory season where we're accessing heaven like never before. Not just positionally, but literally stepping in and coming back. Many supernatural things like near death experiences, visitations, and translations are taking place around the world right now. It's a sign to us at the end of the age.

The first three years of my salvation felt like I was on a rollercoaster. Every time I'd do something that I knew was sin, I'd say,

THE REALM OF EXPECTATION

Something has shifted in the spiritual realm. We're now walking in a revelatory season where we're accessing heaven like never before.

"Oh, I'm not saved," and would ask God to forgive me. With no assurance of my salvation, I agonized in prayer and then tried to read the King James Bible but couldn't understand anything I read. Words like thus, thou, and thine were confusing, and even worse, they started speaking that way in church! Hearing, "Thus sayeth the Lord, I am thy God," I'd think, *I can't even understand the Bible and now you're talking like one.*

The King James Bible English was made up specifically for the Bible; It wasn't the language they spoke in England. When I learned that, I thought, *If it's not obscure enough, make it even harder—why don't you?*

I doggedly read the Bible, and though it wouldn't connect, I knew as a 14-year-old, that it was doing something in my spirit. I could read any other book for hours because I loved to read, but it seemed that when I picked up that Bible, something wasn't working.

At age 17 year when I was baptized in the Holy Spirit, the Word came alive and everything shifted. About a month later while reading 2 Corinthians 12, I felt a great desire to know the supernatural God, not the religious God I had known. I had seen the supernatural when I got saved. Seeing the glory of God on my father's face, I knew God was real, so I went to my room and invited God into my life.

Have a Mindset to Encounter God

I was brought into the Kingdom by an encounter with the Lord's Glory. When I'd go to church and they'd say, "God doesn't do that" I couldn't accept it. Desperate for God, I wanted the supernatural God.

While reading the Bible one day, I came upon 2 Corinthians 12:1: "It is not expedient for me doubtless to glory. I will come to visions and revelations of the Lord" (KJV).

The New King James Version of that passage reads: "It is doubtless not profitable for me to boast. I will come to visions and revelations of the Lord." When I read that, even though it was "out of context, brother," something hit me in my heart as revelation sprang forth. I said, "Lord, I'm going to come to visions and revelations."

It goes on to say: "I know a man in Christ, who was caught up into heaven, whether it was in the body or out of the body, I do not know – God knows – such a one was caught up to the third Heaven" (2 Corinthians 12:2).

He saw and experienced things. No language can convey what I witnessed and experienced. The grace of God in my life from an early age compelled me to desperately desire this.

Scripture says God will give you the desires of your heart.

"Delight yourself also in the Lord, and He shall give you the desires of your heart" (Psalm 37:4).

God birthed this desire in my heart. He said, "I'm going to make you hungry and passionate for the deeper things of the Kingdom." He gave me that passion and answered that passion. Sometimes our prayers can sound like we're making God our servant. "Lord

I want this. Please get it. Lord I want that. Get that for me, too." That's not what Psalm 37:4 means!

"The desires of your heart" means that if you're walking in union with God, He'll birth the desire in you because He's calling you to go into that place. That's why those with a hunger and passion to walk in the supernatural didn't come up with the idea. God did! He put that desire in you because He's calling you into it. This should bring you great comfort!

2 Corinthians 12:1 was a launching pad for me, and it still remains a foundational truth to me: "I will come to visions and revelations of the Lord, whether in the body or out of the body, it doesn't matter. I'm going to encounter God. I will encounter God." That should be your mindset and stance when it comes to the Word of God. Determine that you're not just going read it, you're going to experience it.

Have the Passion to Pursue

> "Thus says the Lord, 'Stand by the ways and see and ask for the ancient paths, where the good way is, and walk in it; And you will find rest for your souls. But they said, 'We will not walk in it'" (Jeremiah 6:16, NASB1995).

I'd been studying, praying, meditating, and practicing when the Lord brought me to this verse. The King James Version is a bit more obscure: "Thus saith the Lord, 'Stand ye in the ways, and see, and ask for the old paths, where is the good way, and walk therein, and ye shall find rest for your souls.' But they said, 'We will not walk therein.'"

When most Christians read, "Thus saith the Lord, 'Stand in the ways'" they think, "Stand in the way." Don't stand in the way!

Move! See and ask for the old paths. He's telling you—commanding you—to see the good way, to walk therein and find rest for your souls.

But they responded, "We will not walk therein." I knew this had something to do with translocation because of the dream my friend Chip had as I shared earlier, but I didn't know where to start. I knew this was speaking about paths, gates, doorways, roads, windows, double doors, etc. Portals are doors and access points. Double doors speak of ingress and egress from the very courts of heaven. When you see double doors in the spirit, know that you're about to have an encounter with the King. You're either stepping into the throne room or He's stepping out of the throne room.

I took this scripture apart in the Hebrew language and did an exhaustive word study. This is how it would read translated directly with the intended meaning. This is what the Lord says, "Stand at the road less traveled and discern."

The road less traveled is the supernatural walk we passionately desire. Most Christians will not walk the road less traveled. Most are comfortable in the tyranny of the familiar, comfortable with the spirit of religion. Religion has a familiarity, and unfortunately, that familiarity breeds contempt for anything unlike it. Most will not make room for the presence of God because they're comfortable with their programs.

The Lord says, "Stand at this road less traveled and discern." The application of the Spirit of God in what He's doing in this moment at this time is to EARNESTLY DESIRE. You must have PASSION to walk in the revelation of translation by faith and passion to bring glory and honor to our Lord. Everything should be done with a passionate desire to bring Him honor.

John 14:15 says, "If ye love me, keep my commandments" (KJV). By keeping His commands, you demonstrate your love for Him, so if you're not keeping His commandments, it proves you don't love Him. Keep His Word and do whatever He speaks to you. Earnestly desire the properly concealed vanishing point.

Elijah told me once, "You have no idea." Elijah understands vanishing points, doesn't he? Earnestly desire the properly concealed vanishing point. This speaks to me on a number of levels. First, I want people to look at me and see Jesus, not Bruce. That's my purpose and my passion.

1 Corinthians 15:31 says, "I protest by your rejoicing which I have in Christ Jesus our Lord, I die daily" (KJV). Dying daily was Paul's passion too as seen in Galatians 2:20: "I have been crucified with Christ; and it is no longer I who live, but Christ lives in me; and the life which I now live in the flesh I live by faith in the Son of God, who loved me and gave Himself up for me (NASB). That's the God-kind of faith! That kind of faith comes as we die daily and learn what it means to die daily.

You have authority to walk in the eternal and perpetual realm. This vanishing point is eternal and perpetual. If you understand quantum physics, you understand light is eternal and perpetual. Light is outside of space and time but interacts with both. Time, space, and light is a construct that God created to house the natural realm.

You have authority to walk in the eternal and perpetual realm. This vanishing point is eternal and perpetual.

The eternal realm of light is not a construct, it's a reality that you're birthed into at the new birth. Your status is far above the construct of the natural realm. You have authority over all the works of God's hands and everything the Lord created fits in the span of His hand, therefore you have authority over the construct. That's why Joshua, under the unction of the Spirit, could say, "Sun, stand still," and it stopped. That's authority over the construct. He interacted with light and interacted with the flow of time.

We like to obscure the Scripture when the Lord says, "At the end of the age, I will shorten the time." Some say that's a metaphor for the fact that things are going to happen quicker. That's an accurate statement, but God is literally going to shorten the time. Research and study on the atomic clock show that what once used to have a 24-hour cycle day, is down to 17 or so hours. This is proven by physics.

We have authority and can walk in an eternal, perpetual realm of light. Because you're created in His image, you have a garment called the flesh but can clothe the flesh with garments of light. This is why Elijah, whom I have encountered several times, carries the glory of God so brightly and that glory is increasing. I told him not long ago in a meeting, "When you pray for people, I want some, too."

In application, the road less traveled looks like this to me: "Lord, where do You want to go today?" "Where do You want to take me?" "Where are we going to translate to?" "Father, send me to the deepest, darkest, most difficult place by Your Spirit, I'll go and do what You want me to do." Ask Him for the assignment of the day and the revelation for the day. Ask and you will receive, that your joy may be full.

God says, "When you ask, journey and vanish, you'll find rest for your soul." In other words, it's not an intellectual, mental assent. It's not something you can figure out or make happen with the intellect.

There's a peace and a rest in your spirit and your soul. You're led of the Spirit. Sometimes your soul will not understand and will ask what you're doing. We've all had those times when the Lord directs us to do something and our mind goes, "What? What? No! That can't be God! That's not logical." His ways are higher than our ways. The logic of heaven doesn't compute with the logic of the natural. God's logic is supernatural logic. In a nutshell, the simple, basic and biblical truth is that if God says it, do it! You don't have to figure it out.

OLAM – TO JOURNEY AND VANISH: ETERNAL AND PERPETUAL

The Hebrew word for journey and vanish is "Olam." It means time out of mind, vanishing point, eternal, and perpetual. Olam is the vanishing point.

I meditated on Olam for months and still do. In the Hebrew, the meaning is encapsulated in each word. If you do the geometric study of the Hebrew, the meaning is even broader. If you study the pictographic significance of the Hebrew letters, you have a volume of revelation on one Scripture that you can study for a lifetime, yet never get the full significance of it. I do this continuously.

As we began walking in translation by faith, Reshma and I would share our experiences in different places. While ministering in Northern Ireland, a brother said, "I have a word for you.

"Yes?" I said.

He said, "Isaiah 58:12-14."

I looked at the verse briefly. It read, "They that shall be of you shall build the old waste places. You shall raise up the foundation of many generations. You'll be called the repairer of the breach, the restorer of paths to dwell in" (Isaiah 58:12).

When I read this, I knew it had something to do with translation, but I was going into a meeting so I tucked it away in my Bible. I had received it in September and then forgot about it. In January, the Lord said, "I gave you a message. Pick it up and look at it."

"Oh, that's right, Lord," I said. "Forgive me." When I opened it up and started a word search of the message, guess what I found?

"They that shall be of you shall rebuild the old OLAM places. Those that you teach will rebuild the OLAM places. Those that you teach are going to restore these ancient paths; the properly concealed vanishing point."

The Lord was saying that you're going to open the road again and you're going to dwell in it. It will be your life. It won't be a "one-off" journey. It'll be a place where you live, move, and have your being consistently in this place.

Don't be underwhelmed. This is a promise to you! Many have wondered, "What's my calling of God?" Well, here it is! One of your callings is to rebuild these properly concealed vanishing points. How do you do it? You start practicing.

The Waste Places

"Korba" is an interesting word that means waste places, drought, or desolation. We're about to take the Word of God, the washing of the water of the Word, and take away drought and bring refreshing to bring newness of life.

Chapter Six

A LIFE OF WORSHIP

THE WORD FROM THE FATHER:

"For you have come to the days of heaven on earth. You've come to a company of great witnesses that have gone before, righteous men made perfect. And in this season, I am combining that which is holy and that which is just and that which is righteous into vessels of flesh. And you shall shine forth in this hour, as one Church both in heaven and on earth, and you shall know the fellowship of the saints. You shall know the worship of heaven. You shall know what it means to walk the streets of gold. For this is the hour of heaven on earth. This is the hour when heaven invades earth. I choose to do that through a company of believers that have yielded themselves to My Spirit. For I will no longer tarry; even now it springs forth."

A WORD ABOUT WORSHIP

Through Spirit-inspired worship, we create a thin place, which means that the fabric between the two dimensions has become so thin that heaven touches earth. In that place I've learned to move and operate. As we share about getting in your prayer chair or into that quiet place with God, I want to caution you that there are no formulas.

I heard an amazing testimony by a woman who was taken before the throne in heaven. She triggered a red light of caution when she talked about somebody giving an instruction to blink 60 times to get a breakthrough into the spirit. No! You don't need to do anything of the sort. An instruction like that becomes a formula. Stay away from formulas! That may indeed be how one individual was led to engage, but that doesn't become a formula for everybody.

We're to be led by His Spirit. In this book we're talking about principles and tools that must fit together with your walk with God. For example, when you have a tool like a wrench, everyone can use it, but it's specifically applied to each person's particular need. I'm sharing principles, not formulas.

LIVE IN A PRINCIPLE OF WORSHIP

As you learn to continually walk in a place of worship, you'll unlock mysteries because worship thins the veil between the seen and the unseen. Psalm 22:3 says, "God inhabits the praises of His people."

Worship means more than singing. Remember the woman with a demon-possessed daughter that came to Jesus in Matthew 15? Scripture says, "Then she worshipped Him saying, 'Lord, help me!'" (Matthew 15:25 NASB).

She was worshipping Him, recognizing the focus of her passion and desire. When you focus your heart on the Lord in a place of worship, it creates a place where encounters happen. Every year

A LIFE OF WORSHIP

Flowing in the spirit of worship leads to the thin place where translations, visions, and other supernatural encounters are released.

on Rosh Hashanah, for the past 17 years, I've had an encounter with God, always from a place of worship.

Waiting on the Lord in worship, with a heart toward God, creates an atmosphere in the spirit where heaven and earth mingle. God inhabits the praise and worship of His people. Psalm 149:6 says, "Let the high praises of God be in their mouth, and a two-edged sword in their hand" (NASB), and Psalm 34:1 says, "I will bless the Lord at all times: his praise shall continually be in my mouth" (KJV). Praise is well defined in Scripture where God provided a key to unlock and walk in the spirit.

Scripture says, "In Him we live and move and have our being" (Acts 17:28). We live and move and have our being through worship. We touch heaven when we worship.

Flowing in the spirit of worship leads to the thin place where translations, visions, and other supernatural encounters are released. For years, Reshma and I led worship in our home 24 hours a day, seven days a week. Apostles, prophets, and others would come into our home and say, "It's so peaceful here! We can feel God's presence here." The atmosphere of worship created the peace when heaven invaded our home.

GOD'S PRESENCE IN WORSHIP

Years ago, we ministered for three nights of meetings in Pennsylvania during Rosh Hashanah. Worship was powerful at those meetings. Live worship is awesome, but one night, however, the profound presence of God came through two hours of CD worship music. I've never witnessed anything like it before or after that. The heart of the people brought the atmosphere of His presence. If the stones can cry out, we can qualify also! (Luke 19:40)

The Rise of God's Army

During one of those meetings, we entered into worship when I suddenly saw a five-foot flaming sword appear. "Lord, what is that?" I asked.

The Lord didn't answer me.

We worshiped for two hours when finally, the Lord spoke. "Take it!" He said. Putting my hand out, I grabbed the sword. My hand locked onto the hilt of the sword and I couldn't let go for two more hours of worship!

Because I had to sit down to rest for a moment, I laid the sword across my lap. When it touched and burned me, I jumped back up and said, "Lord, what am I supposed to do with this?"

"Sheath the sword," He instructed. When He spoke those words, I received the revelation. We hide the Word of God in our heart, so when I sheathed the sword, a fire started in my heart and pulsed throughout my body.

I was then translated out of the room and was standing in a vast, open plain somewhere on planet earth. I looked down and saw that I was clothed in the armor of God. It wasn't flashy, brilliant or glorious but dull grey in color. Grey speaks of the humility that comes with maturity.

Looking to my left, I realized that I was in a formation line with every head turning in unison. As we turned our heads forward, I saw light, life, and glory as far as the eye could see. The light darkened increasingly until it became obvious that the people furthest from the light and in darkness had changed. They dragged about, some in such heavy bondage that they could barely move. Demons covered and surrounded these people, riding and brutalizing them. A horrific sight! We stood quietly, yet didn't move as the King had not given the command.

This is a vital lesson to us. We shouldn't take action when we think or believe we can do something, but instead, we should act when God instructs us to act.

> "Therefore Jesus answered and was saying to them, 'Truly, truly, I say to you, the Son can do nothing of Himself, unless it is something He sees the Father doing; for whatever the Father does, these things the Son also does in like manner'" (John 5:19 NASB).

We all stood ready to go, until we heard the command: "Draw forth your sword!" As one, we drew forth our swords! A wave of glory blew through us and destroyed the darkness, the chains, and the demons. The people arose from that place of darkness as if they had awoken from a dark sleep. It seemed as if they hadn't realized that they'd been in bondage.

As they looked at us and saw the light, they ran toward us and joined the ranks of the army of God.

The Lord said, "March!" and as one we moved across the face of the earth. Seeing darkness turn to light, with every step, a redemptive anointing redeemed that which had been fallen and under the curse.

Because I spent 10 years in the military, I asked the Lord, "Lord, in every army the soldiers get tired from the battle. Where is the place of furlough? Where do they go when they need rest?"

Instantly, I found myself in Paradise. In awe, I saw things impossible to describe. The air in heaven is alive! Everything is alive. You can talk to the grass, the trees, and the animals. You can talk to the fruit you eat and the water you drink because it's alive! Nothing is inanimate and all interacts and is filled with life, understanding, wisdom, and intelligence.

In a distance I could see a little boy reaching up to grab a piece of fruit off of a tree. As the boy reached up, the branch holding the fruit pulled away to tease him. Then they laughed together!

I also saw a little girl that stood on tiptoes, unable to reach the fruit on a tree. The tree branch bent down and handed her the fruit! I saw families, friends, and others mingling and enjoying Paradise with such joy and effusive love.

The love I witnessed grabbed me as it flowed like waves. The very air was saturated with a quality of love that we don't comprehend. We've had touches of this love from the Lord, but that's filtered through our flesh, so we haven't had the full impact of this love, as His love is life.

In a distance I saw the City of God, which as Scripture says, is 1,500 miles square and 1,500 miles tall. The highest satellite orbiting the earth is only 200 miles up. When the City of God comes to earth, you'll see and experience the scope and grandeur of which I'm speaking.

The love I witnessed grabbed me as it flowed like waves. The very air was saturated with a quality of love that we don't comprehend.

To my left was a small tributary from the River of Life. "Lord," I said. "What is that?"

"It's an offshoot of the River of Life called the River of Revelation," He said.

"Oh," I said, noticing a cup.

"Go ahead and drink," the Lord told me. I walked over to the river, grabbed the cup, dipped it in, and drank. Revelation hit my spirit in an indescribable overwhelming way, reminding me of the massive data downloads you might see on a computer screen in the movies.

Shaking, I said, "Dear God! Lord! How do I remember all of this?"

"You don't have to remember," He said. "It's now a part of you."

Wow! I thought.

The Lord said, "Put your hand out." As I followed His direction, a tree above me dropped a piece of fruit. "Eat!" He said. "In the days that are directly in front of you, this is where the Church, My people, can come to find refreshing to continue the journey. Now go back and tell them." Immediately I found myself back in the room.

Stay in Worship

You have access to all things because of the blood of Jesus. When the Holy Spirit reminded me of this truth, I said, "Lord, I need a refreshing!"

As I spoke those words, I was transported back to that place where I was empowered by that refreshing. The Lord said, "Help yourself!"

We usually travel a minimum of 10 months of the year. Always moving, it seems as if our second home is a suitcase, so we need the refreshing.

That level of refreshing comes through worship by an atmosphere created in the hearts of those who desire to connect with God. And when you go, you never have to leave that place!

Genesis 28:12 says that the ladder Jacob saw went from earth to heaven. This starts with you. Staying in worship throughout the day is as simple as saying, "Father, I love You." Or, "Lord, help me. I can't do this." The Lord has been teaching me that if I learn to submit myself daily to Him and resist the devil, the devil will flee and God will come nearer. That truth has taken me even deeper.

I've made it a daily practice to say, "Lord, I submit myself to You. All that I am or hope to be, my past, hopes dreams, wishes, desires and needs, I submit everything to You, God. I submit my successes and failures, my members, thoughts, imagination and life to You. I surrender everything to You." Then I continue: "Now, Lord, I resist the devil and because I resist him, he must flee. I choose to draw near to You, Father, and I thank You, Father, that You draw near to me." Then I walk with God throughout that day. That's worship.

After prayer, the Lord says, "You can go deeper still."

"Really? How?" I ask.

He says, "It's time for My people to learn to live from heaven to earth." Scripture says that God has given spiritual and natural gifts to every man. To live from heaven to earth, daily surrender that which you consider your spiritual and natural gifts.

Worship as the Act of Surrendering 100% to God

If you tell the Lord, "Lord, today I choose to administrate heaven on earth from my heavenly position," something will begin to shift. For example, if you have the gift of prophecy and surrendered it to God, saying, "Lord, I don't want to walk in the gift of prophecy. I want to walk with the Prophet of the gift, Jesus," something shifts and you enter into a realm of walking in something far greater. It's like a quantum leap shift.

If you want to learn to walk in the spirit, translate, and have visions, understand that I'm giving you keys that have been years in the making. My ceiling is your floor. Take the "keys" and make them a habit!

> Jesus said, "I can of mine own self do nothing: as I hear, I judge: and my judgment is just; because I seek not mine own will, but the will of the Father which hath sent me" (John 5:30 KJV).

Do you realize that you can't even take a breath without God? If He removed grace, the world would vanish. If He canceled His Word, we'd vaporize and—poof—be gone. We can do nothing without God. His influence and His Word uphold all things. This is worship and what Jesus was doing when He said, "I can of My own self, do nothing. I am totally 100% reliant and dependent upon You, Father. And I'll do what I see You do and I'll say what I hear You say." Anything other than that is fleshly dead works.

Moving from where we are—or where we think we are—in the things of the Spirit, to where we can be, will be a bit of a bumpy road, because we must navigate beyond our understanding and intellect to recognize our absolute complete dependence upon the

Do you realize that you can't even take a breath without God? If He removed grace, the world would vanish. If He canceled His Word, we'd vaporize and—poof—be gone.

Lord. In that place of dependence is freedom and liberty. I often tell the Lord, "Lord, I give up!" Quitting? No! I quit using the arm of the flesh and rely on God. If He doesn't do it, it's not going to get done.

It took me over 20 years to learn these truths. After getting saved at age 14, I carried a lot of baggage, acquired traits, and generational leanings with me into the Kingdom.

Not to disparage my parents in any way, but both of my parents were raised in an atmosphere of absolute rejection, betrayal, and abandonment, so they brought rejection, betrayal and abandonment into their relationship. You can only give what you've got. Of course, they loved us, but their love was covered up with the baggage. They didn't realize their baggage was powerfully affecting and subverting their love for us.

Being told at a young age (until age 14) "You're no good, you'll never amount to anything, you're going to end up in jail" was the expression of my father's love. He thought what he considered to be strong love would motivate me, but instead it almost destroyed me.

When my dad got saved, it absolutely shocked me the next time I came to him for a dressing down. "You're better than that," he said. "You can do better."

I remember thinking, "What is this? Is my dad in there somewhere?" Something shifted in me after that. What had been built into me from babyhood until age 14 took years to get free from as the Lord delivered me from the scheme of rejection, betrayal, and abandonment.

We all bring baggage into our Christian walk and all face challenges that God allows in our life to perfect our Christlike character. We can't do it on our own; it requires 100% dependence on God. Passion and hunger for Him is the gift He gives you to get you there. When passion and hunger are released more eloquently through worship toward God, breakthrough comes.

I stumbled, fell, and faltered; at times feeling defeated the first 15-20 years of my Christian walk. Wondering if I'd ever get anywhere in God, I'd spend hours crying out to God. "Oh God, forgive me!" I'd pray. "I don't want to fail You. I really don't want to fail You!"

Though I'd been told I was a failure throughout my life, breakthrough finally came. I was delivered and my life completely transformed.

I continued to resist using my wisdom, my strength, and my understanding for so long. I was told to quote Scripture, so I quoted Scripture. Being told I must say, "Forgive me," so many times, I said, "Forgive me," so many times. When told I had to repeatedly say "Thank-you" to the Lord, I did that as well.

Realizing that formulas didn't work, I threw it all away and said, "God, help me! Oh, God! Please help me! If you don't help me, I'm going to perish!" I was broken and had come to the end of myself. Thank God for that or I'd be stuck in the past right now.

Part of the process for me to see and walk in the spirit was telling the Lord, "God, I give up. Why can't I get free? What are You saying?"

He said, "I've been waiting for 20 years for you to ask that." Responding to my cry for help, He told me exactly what to do, including confession and repentance. As I obeyed the Lord, breakthrough came! 20 years of formulas and religious protocol were gone! I despise religion as religion kept me in bondage. One word from God, however, set me free. And I'm free indeed!

This is why I reiterate the importance of dialoguing with God: "Father, what are You saying about this? Father, what are

You saying? What are You doing?" Asking Him these questions will save years of struggle. Simply asking, "Father, what are You saying today?" will keep you from the mercy of religious protocol. When someone is standing before you who needs ministry, if you ask, "Father, what are You saying?" He'll give you the answer. That's how Jesus walked. He did only what He saw the Father doing.

We learn to walk in the spirit through absolute dependence on God and listening to His voice. God's voice is not just words. One third of the Bible came through visions and dreams, which are also His voice. When you receive a dream, that's God speaking to you. When you have a vision, that's also God speaking to you. As a lover of God, you'll learn how to decipher what He's communicating by asking questions. Everything we experience, we dialogue with the Lord and say, "Lord, define that for us. Give us understanding." Occasionally, God answers by supernaturally downloading the word of knowledge.

Visitation of Archangel Michael

When we recently had a spiritual visitation of Michael the Archangel in a school in the Philippines, it became clear to me that we're in a time of breakthrough. Michael was there to help break down the barriers that have kept people from walking in the translation by faith revelation. When we pay heed to laying down our own agenda and plans, heaven intervenes. I had just told the Lord in that meeting that I had nothing apart from what He could give, and He said, "Good! Michael's here for breakthrough."

The spirit of worship saturated the atmosphere and created an entry into the supernatural for us. This day and hour of visitation

We learn to walk in the spirit through absolute dependence on God and listening to His voice.

came upon those passionately seeking Him. Much focus and attention by the Church throughout the earth will be about what God is doing in places with a hunger for God.

Hear this and hear this loud and clear: Guard what God is giving you. Steward it well, because every "flim-flam" man and religious spirit will try to take it, warp it, and use it for something that is not of God. Don't allow that! Be bold enough to chase them off, in love. Jealously guard the gifts God has bestowed upon you, and don't let anything get in the way.

Jesus was not a pacifist, yet He was meek. Meekness is not weakness, but power under control and yielded to the Spirit of God. God told Jesus to, "Make a scourge and chase them from the temple."

Sometimes I've prayed, "Oh, God, can I do that, too? Please! Just once!" But that's my flesh. Don't let the world steal what God is doing through an explosion in the things of the spirit.

Jesus is walking the streets of cities throughout the world. Spontaneous visitations and salvations are springing forth now because of the prayers and worship of God's people. He's going to call to you in the night season, during times of worship, and call in times of prayer to show you what He's about to do. You need to go there and be a part of it!

"But I have a job," you might say. You have a calling higher than your job. "I can't just walk out," we might reason. Listen intently:

If God tells you to do it, drop it all and run. He'll take care of the details. Don't do this foolishly, but circumspectly obey the voice of God. Favor will accompany what God instructs us to do.

In this hour we'll see a visitation in the political arena. That which has been tainted and darkened by the spirit of this age is about to come to the light. Get ready for revival in the presidential palaces. As bold as some leaders have been for darkness, they'll become twice as bold for light.

You have a destiny and purpose beyond your wildest dreams or comprehension. It's time to see. There's a grace on me to pray for your spiritual eyes. Read the following prayer I'm releasing by faith, and then place your hands on your eyes in agreement.

Prayer for Your Spiritual Eyes

"Father, according to the grace that is upon me, and the leading of Ruach Hakodesh, I command the scales to be removed from their spiritual eyes. So, Father, as they choose to engage, their eyes will be opened. Even right now, Father, I ask that their eyes will be opened and they'll see in a way they've never seen before. And Lord, according to this grace, I'm also asking that the scales would be removed from their natural eyes too, as You heal their natural eyesight. Lord, I thank You for what You're doing. I give You praise. I give You glory and honor. Selah. Thank You, Father. Thank You, Father. Thank You, Father."

Stay in a place of rest right now. Close your eyes, lay your hands on them and thank the Lord. Start saying, "Whatever it takes, Lord." Focus everything within you on Him.

A Prayer to Remove Blocking and Hindering Things

"Father, I pull down the stronghold of religion upon the lives of these individuals. Hidden practices that they don't realize they walk in. I break off the chains of religious bondage they don't know that are upon them. Father, I remove the need to be recognized by men. I break that off their hearts and lives. I release them from the scheme of rejection, betrayal, and abandonment in their hearts right now. I see them free to worship You, in the fullness of who You created them to be. I release them, Lord. I break them free of the witchcraft that has come against them. Even generationally, it's broken and you'll go back whence you came. Psalm 109:17-20 says, "They that love cursing, let it come upon them." We release it back to where it came from. They are covered in Your blood. Father, even now, as they're free, the generation that came forth through them are free. Their children are free. Their grandchildren are free. They're in a place of grace where visitation is released. Thank You, Father. Thank You, Father."

Right now, I'm seeing that this revelation about translation by faith is not a great light in the Church or with pastors and leaders. But a great glory is coming, and people are going to be drawn to those buildings of worship out of curiosity. Some of them will not even know, but they're going to come in because of the brightness of the shining of the glory of God. When they get there, they're going to see it all over the people. This is the season of great harvest. But it's going to be unlike anything you've witnessed. It's not going to come through the handing out of tracts and profound preaching. God Himself is going to draw them in as they yield themselves to Him.

There's a strength coming to your mortal bodies, especially to those who are a bit older, because the Lord will empower you to finish the course. You're going to run the race and the finish line is not death, the finish line is the catching away. Release them, Father.

Chapter Seven

FOLLOW THE FORERUNNERS

As we learn to walk in translation by faith, we learn also that God has already had people walking in this throughout each generation. These forerunners can encourage and teach us on our own journey.

I want to introduce you to Brother Grubbs, a forerunner in this generation. Brother Grubbs was in his late 60s when our good friend, Dr. Flo Ellers, interviewed him in 1987. Our friend had heard about Brother Grubbs, who testified that he had been translating throughout the world for over 30 years. Two angels would come to pick Brother Grubbs up and take him various places on earth to minister the Gospel.

In these times of translation, his wife and family would sometimes see a bright flash, and then he'd vanish. At other times, she'd see nothing but his clothes left in the bed. Sometimes he'd call from other countries and say, "I won't be home tonight," and he'd tell her where he was ministering.

After Dr. Flo learned about him, she and her husband scheduled a visit to talk with and do a videotaped interview of Brother Grubbs and his wife. Back in 1987, the subject of translation by faith was way over the top, so Dr. Flo kept that video under wraps until 2003, when she heard Reshma and me speaking about translocation.

Dr. Ellers approached us and said, "I have something for you," and gave us the video interview. We digitized it and put it on DVD so we could release it to those with whom we felt led to share it. Unfortunately, someone put the content on the Internet without regard to copyright laws. I highly recommend that you research Brother Grubbs and his testimony, as it will confirm what God is doing in this age.

The following is a transcript of a small piece of that interview:

Interviewer: This article was sent to me by Sister Gwen Shaw from the End Time Handmaidens called "Stranger at the UN." It's an excerpt of an article that appeared in a magazine, regarding a message given by Paul Harvey. He was a nationally known news analyst over the network of the American Broadcasting Company on Christmas Eve, 1950. This article talks about a man who was translated, who appeared in the UN, and brother Grubbs tells us that he is the man who was translated into the UN.

Brother Grubbs, you tell [sic] me that you have had a stroke—several strokes—since then, which have impaired your memory somewhat, but can you share with us what you do recall of this happening that was written in "Stranger at the UN?"

Brother Grubbs: Well, I can remember some of it. Just a little of it.

When I went in, they had guards. I mean, they had them all around. They were, I would say, six foot apart, facing out from the building all around where the doors were, of course, because you couldn't get in anywhere else anyhow. All the doors had three guards on each side of each door facing out. You couldn't get in unless you had a pass or something to verify who you were and had the right to go in. Well, I walked in. So, I wasn't even visible. They didn't see me. I went in and went down. It was a walkway that went down with wide wooden steps. It was a ramp-like affair down to the main arena affair-like, 'cause it was the bleachers or whatever you want to call it, down the main floor where the speaker was to be up on the big platform.

I walked down that. Nobody said a word. Nothing was said until I was about halfway down, and some guy hollered at me and said, "Hey! Who are you?"

I remember that, and I turned around and said, "It's none of your business!" I remember doing that.

He said, "Hey! Come here!" I paid no attention and went on down.

When I got down to the bottom of the ramp, there was a seat right next to the aisle and I sat down, right next to a man. He put his hand on my knee like this and he said, "Welcome, buddy!" I don't know to this day who he was, but I have a notion that I think I know who it was—one of God's angels. He was dressed in a suit. You know, you take an angel, most of them was always in white apparel, but this guy's dressed in a suit. He said, "Welcome, buddy!"

Well, when he bothered me and after that was all over with, he walked up the ramp with me and we walked on out. When we got up to the top and went out the door, there was the officer who'd confronted us and he said, "Hey, I hollered at you. Who are you?"

After I gave him my name, he said, "How did you get in?"

"That's a good question," I said. "You answer it." He looked and he stopped me, looking all around while I was still standing there. I'm not going to say what he said because it wasn't very nice.

I don't understand why I was there. I really don't understand why I was there. If there was a reason for me being [there], I don't know or remember what it was. Maybe it was to show them something and then to realize that something could happen and they wouldn't know it until it was too late, that somebody could get in and they wouldn't catch them in time or what, I don't know. But that guy made that dirty, nasty, filthy remark, and I was standing right there, but he couldn't see me nor the one with me, and I'm not transparent.

Interviewer: Did you examine your body? Were there any changes in your body? Anything supernatural?

Brother Grubbs: Not that I recall, Sis. Now, either it happened to him or the Lord made me invisible so he couldn't see me. I don't know what happened.

Sister Grubbs: Sometimes, they took him in the body. Sometimes, they took him just in the spirit and his body is here.

Brother Grubbs: Now, I don't know whether God can take a spirit and make it physically appearing or not.

This is just a small part of Brother Grubbs' life and testimony. I again highly encourage you to watch the entire interview, as it will blow open some doors as to possibilities in the Kingdom, especially concerning translation.

I must add that when they vanished, the man who'd sat next to him, (the angel), vanished with him. The police officer was so frightened, he began to curse, which is when he knew it was an angel.

This type of experience was everyday life for Brother Grubbs. He's gone home to be with the Lord now, but his testimony remains. Last year, we received an email from a longtime neighbor of Brother Grubbs in Portland, Oregon, who said, "Thank you for making that video of Brother Grubbs available. We used to watch him vanish, and we're glad somebody is finally giving him the honor that was due him, because the Church totally ostracized him."

Brother and Sister Grubbs were wounded and ostracized by the Church over this. They couldn't darken the door of the Church in that area because people said he was of the devil. He led many people to come into the Kingdom and he was a forerunner.

Brother Grubb sowed seed. He provided a floor from which you can launch. God is releasing multitudes of His people to walk in the same level of revelation and power. Are you one of them?

A Word from Reshma Allen

I want to share how my journey of translation by faith started and grew:

I grew up in the Fiji Islands and attended Bible College for about four years where I acquired a lot of head knowledge about the things of God. Though I had studied God's Word and read the supernatural stories in the Bible, I never imagined that those experiences could happen to me. I had learned much about the Lord but had made no supernatural connection.

From the time I was a little girl, I've had many dreams. My family thought I was possessed because I'd see end-time events and would share them with my family. I didn't understand until about 15 years ago, when I started receiving revelation about the dreams, learning what they meant, how the Lord uses dreams and why He was showing me things through dreams.

When Bruce and I were first married, we'd go to different places around the world to minister, and I would witness God doing amazing works. Suddenly, people would ask me questions like, "What do you see? What do you hear? Do you see like your husband sees?"

I thought about these questions because I was nervous in the beginning and wouldn't talk to people. I love people, but I wouldn't stand in front of people to minister because I thought American Christians knew everything. *What do I have that they would need to hear from me?* I thought. I was just a girl from a tiny little island in the middle of nowhere, right?

At meetings, when Bruce ministered, things would happen, and he'd ask me, "Did you hear that? Did you see that? Did you feel that?"

I'd say, "What? What are you talking about?" I'd sat there like I was spiritually dead for a long time. As I pondered people's questions, I made a determination in my heart: *I know it's in Scripture. It's written in black and white. God does this, and it belongs to me, too.* Seeing this truth, I went home and said to the Lord, "God, here I am. I will see. I will hear, and I will engage in the supernatural because it belongs to me."

I didn't lie to the people but explained that I didn't see like my husband saw and didn't feel like he felt. The attitude of our heart is important. I could have lied, I could have been jealous of my husband and could have made up stories, but I didn't. "No, I don't," I said in honesty. "Not yet, but I will!" That's when things started changing for me. As I started praying like that in my study time and making myself available to the Lord, I began to feel and see differently.

When we go to meetings, Bruce doesn't usually tell me what he's going to speak about. I'd ask him, "Honey, what are you speaking about today?"

He'd say, "From the Bible."

"Okay," I'd say, "I will pray."

I'd close my eyes during the meetings and say to the Lord, "Lord, I yield my senses to You, I yield the members of my body to You. Please, show me what's going on." In response to my prayer, the Lord started showing me things in the room and I'd see a vision of what Bruce was going to speak about. Then, if somebody in the room had health issues or pain in their body, I'd feel it in my body. I'd also experience emotions others were experiencing.

When I first started receiving words of knowledge, I wouldn't say anything but later would tell my husband about it. "Why didn't you tell me?" Bruce would ask. "That's a word of knowledge! Somebody was suffering from that." Then he added, "Tell me when you see or hear."

At first, I said, "You tell them." So, he'd share the word and I wouldn't stand up. Yet when he shared the words God was giving me, I'd see the results, which encouraged me. I eventually said, "I can do this!" and started to stand up and deliver the words of knowledge.

God will use you in this way also. The Bible says that when a little child comes to his earthly father and asks for bread, the father does not give him a stone (Matthew 7:9). We're asking our eternal Father for revelation and understanding, so He gives us these things and shows us what to do.

God Uses Us as We Sleep

While ministering in the state of Wisconsin in the U.S., I (Reshma) had a vivid dream one night where I found myself on a beach somewhere. Going up and down the beach, I warned the people of coming danger, then took them to a higher ground. In the middle of the dream, I got up during the night to use the bathroom, and when I returned to bed and fell asleep, I was immediately back in that dream.

Throughout the night, this experience seemed real. The next morning, I said to Bruce, "I really feel like I need to turn the TV on to see what's going on." Shocked to discover that a tsunami had just hit Japan, I realized that my nighttime experience was more than just a dream. It had not only happened, but I was there! One young man in this vivid dream was so scared that he froze and couldn't move, so I took him by the hand and led him to higher ground.

God can use us in our sleep. When we go to bed, we can say, "Lord, use me even in my sleep." We've determined in our ministry to say, "Lord, give us a group of people that would be first responders for You, so whenever there's a need in the world, we'll translate

God can use us in our sleep. When we go to bed, we can say, "Lord, use me even in my sleep."

to the location to bring needed help and see lives changed and saved." I believe that God is preparing a group of people to do this, and you can be part of it!

Dreams and Visions

I dreamed of being in a place with a woman and her two little girls. One child was in the house in a drum of water. I didn't understand what that meant. The other little girl was outside with her mother, who was doing ungodly things that she shouldn't have been doing as her child watched.

Seeing this scene troubled me. I thought, *This child shouldn't be watching what's going on here.* Suddenly, I had both little girls and had taken them to a place where I played with and cared for them.

Next, I was in a building full of activities and children where some kind of preparation was taking place. I brought the girls to this house, which was a safe place. After sending them to be with the other children, I saw a woman. "Can I help you?" I asked her. "Can I do something to help you prepare?"

"Yes!" she said. She explained that outside was an empty garden that needed to be planted and made beautiful because within one week, a judging would take place. People would be coming from all over the world to see and judge this garden.

"We want to get the first prize," she told me.

"I'm going to help you," I said.

I started thinking, *I really want to help these people, because I do love gardening.* My Facebook page is graced with pictures of flowers at our house in the summertime. With a love for flowers, I said to myself, *I'm going to help these people prepare this garden and we're going to win!*

When I came to the front of the house and looked up, suddenly I saw the Lord standing there. I ran over to Him, held onto His legs and said, "Please, Lord, give me ideas to make this garden so we can win the prize." In this beautiful place I was suddenly covered with gold dust—layers and layers of sparkles all over my body.

As I prepared the garden, I turned my eyes as two people—Bruce and I—appeared. Although I was in the dream, I also saw myself entering into the garden as we were ready to work in the garden.

As I prayed and asked God for understanding, I believe this dream is connected to the school of translation, (School of the Supernatural), because when we teach these revelations about translation, we're with those who need to be taught. We're studying and learning from the Lord as we prepare. God has provided a special grace for preparation in this season.

As Bruce and I have traveled around the world, we've seen pockets of people that hunger for the things of God. Their hunger and passion for the Lord have resulted in supernatural happenings. Some readers are going places and are forerunners in this garden the Lord is preparing. The eyes of the world are going to see it! Thank you for allowing us in your garden. We're so excited to be a part of your journey.

INTERPRETATION OF THE DREAM BY BRUCE ALLEN

The mother with the two daughters speaks of the Church. The girl in the barrel of water is one that immerses herself in the washing of the water of the Word. The other girl was carnal, following the leading of the mother who was mixing and desecrating herself with the things of the world.

This is the garden of the Lord. We're all the planting of the Lord, and the Lord is saying that it's time to invest in this garden so you win the prize. Judgment is not coming from the world. There's one Judge who we want to hear say, "Well done, good and faithful servant!"

The world will take note of what is happening. Not only are Reshma and I privileged to be a part of your journey (your garden) but God will bring others along to help to plant and grow this garden in this season. It's going to spring forth, just as Reshma said. This will happen in a short period of time. Seven is the number of rest and covenant promise fulfillment. God is going to do this quickly.

Michael Van Vlymen started walking in the truths taught in this book after hearing instruction in my book *Gazing into Glory*, and through video teachings like the ones presented on Sid Roth's television program, "It's Supernatural." Michael's wife, Gordana, who is passionate for the things of God, is being used in these ways. Here's a peak into her journey:

A Word from Gordana Van Vlymen

Gordana Van Vlymen was born again in 1986 and got to know the Holy Spirit who became her best friend. She testifies that the Holy Spirit has allowed her to experience and witness many supernatural events. Gordana used to read about healings and other supernatural encounters in the Bible, and though she and her husband Mike visited different churches and ministries, she didn't see a display of what the Bible talked about. She was never satisfied because she knew something was missing.

In 2011, she told the Lord, "This is it, Lord. I'm just giving up. I'm going back to the faith I was brought up in." Gordana was an Orthodox Christian from Macedonia (former republic of Yugoslavia), where the majority of Christians are of that background.

On this particular day, Mike and Gordana were attending a healing conference in Missouri with Bill Johnson and Randy Clark. Though she says it was a great meeting, she was crying out to God on the inside. Mike didn't know it, but she said to God, "This is it. I'm never going back to church again. All of these things that I believe but don't see are going to be put on the shelf." She cried out in desperation because although she knew the supernatural was real, what she read in the Word and what she saw in the church weren't the same thing.

On that day, November 11th, 2011, (11/11/11) the Lord heard her cry and answered that cry. The Lord literally put His hand inside her chest and started shaking her on the inside. She was a little afraid of what was happening because she had never experienced something like this before. She had seen this shaking happen to people on TV, but she says it's not the same when you experience it yourself.

The shaking continued throughout the night. Anybody who came close to her, touched her, or tried to hold her would get slain in the Spirit. She didn't understand at all what was happening.

When she and Mike returned home, she had to hide what she was experiencing because her family had never seen anything like this. Her mom and their children live with them and, like them, they had no grid for this encounter.

She ran upstairs to hide because she felt something bubbling up from the inside. She kept her mouth closed and placed her hand over her mouth hoping that nothing would escape. Feeling as if she might explode, she suddenly started speaking Chinese very loudly, and because she couldn't control it, she closed the door to their bedroom.

From that night on, the Lord has been taking her places throughout the world every night to minister. He often allowed her to preach, sing, and worship in China where she saw multitudes of people. During one of the trips while preaching to the crowds, they all started running because the police were coming after them. Gordana is normally very shy, so for her to preach before large crowds, speaking and singing in Chinese, is surely the Lord's work.

As it turned out, their kids weren't scared of these supernatural encounters. These experiences were the beginning of the supernatural happenings the Lord was doing with her and through her as she surrendered herself to Him. "Whatever You want to do, Lord," she told God, "do it. It doesn't matter to me how foolish I look."

For four or five years, they couldn't have anybody over to their house because of what the Lord was doing through her. Maybe one day the Lord will allow her to share everything.

The Lord has taken Gordana many places by the spirit including Italy and Israel. She knew where she was because of the smell of the foods in various locations. She's also visited heaven, where she heard and sang with the choir.

When she was born again, because of the hurt and pain she had experienced, the Lord put His hand on her heart. She says it felt like what I shared when the Lord gave me the sword: It burned and burned. She didn't feel pain, only love, as God healed her heart.

Gordana always knows when God is around her. He lets her see the angels, which she's seen around the house in a natural body. She's also seen the two angels, one tall and the other a bit shorter, who accompany her everywhere.

If you yield your body, soul and spirit, Gordana says, God will use you and take you places. She says, as Reshma said, "Prepare yourself! He's going to do great and mighty works through you."

Chapter Eight

THE EYES OF YOUR UNDERSTANDING ENLIGHTENED

DEVELOPING VISUAL CAPACITY THROUGH SANCTIFIED IMAGINATION

I'd like to clearly define the sanctified imagination: The sanctified imagination is the bridge from the natural to the spiritual realm. In order to perceive and walk in an open heaven, you must develop a visual capacity.

Let me share a story about my younger brother, Troy, who was born with cerebral palsy and brain damaged at birth. Doctors told my parents that Troy would never walk, talk or have an education, yet my Dad would never accept that. A driven man, Dad was a successful businessman and anything he touched became prosperous. Because of his success, he could afford the best doctors and care money could buy.

By age 10, Troy was walking, talking, attending school and getting an education. In a sense, my Dad won, feeling as if, "I can do anything." When Troy died in a drowning accident, my parents were totally devastated. Dad started drinking after realizing he had to confront something like Troy's death, which he could do nothing about.

When you have a special needs brother, sister, son or daughter, you learn how to love the unlovely. My parents loved Troy fiercely, and when he was gone, they were broken. Dad tried—unsuccessfully—to cover the hurt with alcohol.

Nine months later, when somebody invited Dad to a luncheon, he thought, *Maybe I can get a Chaser to get rid of this hangover.* What he didn't hear was that Full Gospel Businessmen were hosting the luncheon.

At the Full Gospel Businessmen's luncheon, Dad surrendered his heart to Jesus which changed our entire family and led ultimately to millions of people around the world being saved.

One day the Lord said, "You know, your brother fulfilled his destiny."

"What do you mean, Lord?" I asked.

"Troy was a seed and he fulfilled his destiny," the Lord answered. Because of his faithfulness into that which he was called, millions of people call Jesus "Lord" today.

As an evangelist, Dad impacted thousands of churches where hundreds of thousands of people were saved and miracles beyond description took place. Dad's ministry had a snowball effect because many of those people then entered the ministry and won the lost also.

In the natural realm, because of the fallen condition of humankind, sons and daughters can be born with birth defects. But when one is born again, there are no birth defects, as in the realm of the spirit all senses are intact. You have eyes to see, ears to hear, and a nose to smell and discern.

THE EYES OF YOUR UNDERSTANDING ENLIGHTENED

Handicapped children of God do not exist except for those who refuse to exercise their senses and develop their spiritual capacity. They go through this life handicapped because of ignorance, tradition, religion, or unbelief, failing to engage what God has placed within them.

This is why we must be a people of the Word of God, adhering to Scripture and believing His Word more than we believe our physical senses or the word of man. Take anything communicated to you back to the Word to see if it's God's final say on the matter.

If we study Scripture with our spiritual senses, we'll discover important keys. In John 3:3 Jesus said, "Truly, I say to you, except a man is born again, he cannot see the Kingdom of God." He's communicating that if you're born again, you can see. "See" in the Greek and Aramaic is not just posturing, a metaphor, or a perception only (although it can be a perception). It literally speaks of seeing into the realm of the Kingdom of God. I like that!

This truth was initially a challenge for me as I had to learn to rise above the religious instruction to lay hold of the reality of Scripture. Every time I'd grab hold of a scriptural truth, I'd go to leaders, elders, or professors to ask questions. Unfortunately, I was always discouraged in my desire to move toward the supernatural God that exists. They wanted me to stay with the logical God that they could understand. They kept telling me, "No you can't. He doesn't. He won't," all words of doubt and unbelief.

In John 3:3 Jesus said, "Truly, I say to you, except a man is born again, he cannot see the Kingdom of God." He's communicating that if you're born again, you can see.

At first, I'd get frustrated and angry, but then I began to understand. We become imprisoned, snared, and in bondage to what we believe. You're either in bondage to what you believe or are liberated by what you believe in the Word. As for me, I kept going after God!

Luke 24:16 says, "They were unaware that it was Jesus walking alongside them, for God prevented them from recognizing him" (TPT). The story of the road to Emmaus is one of my favorite passages in Scripture as it speaks of "early in the morning of the third day." Prophetically, we're in that time, "early in the morning of the third day," because according to 2 Peter 3:8, a day is a thousand years.

"Their eyes were restrained so they didn't know Him" (Luke 24:16).

There they were, having just witnessed the passion of the Christ, the crucifixion, the death and burial. After the women from the garden tomb told them that Jesus had risen from the dead, His two disciples were walking along discussing these most unusual events. Scripture says that Jesus came alongside them, yet they didn't recognize Him. Think about this! They were disciples of the Lord who had walked with Him for three and a half years. Now He's risen from the dead and they don't recognize Him!

I've heard many interesting thoughts on why they didn't recognize Jesus. Some say He had a glorified body, yet they would surely have recognized that. Others say His visage was marred, which means He was brutalized and unrecognizable. They'd seen that already, so I doubt they'd have been walking along and talking to somebody that ghastly and ugly, yet not recognize Him.

So, what kept them from recognizing Jesus? Luke 24:21 offers the clue: "But we were hoping that it was He who was going to redeem Israel. Indeed, besides all this, today is the third day since these things happened."

Talking back and forth, they said, "And we were hoping that He was the One to come." Their preconceived ideas, theology, eschatology, if you will, blinded them to the reality of who God was.

We must remain teachable. None of us know Him as we ought to know Him. Nobody corners the market on revelation, and no movement should claim to corner the market on revelation, and can say, "We've got it and we're the only ones who are right." If you hear that coming from any pulpit, run! We must walk with humility and remain teachable so our eyes can remain open to see.

There's good news! In Luke 24:31, their eyes were opened and they knew Him. I love this because Emmaus means to be hot from sunrise to sunset. The moment you make a choice to move toward consistent passion, Jesus Himself comes alongside, opens the Word, and explains everything in Scripture concerning Himself.

Do you want a visitation from Jesus? Stay on the road of passion, as that's the key. Jesus had tested His disciples, and when they finally reached Emmaus, He tested them again. He acted as if He was going to keep going, yet they constrained Him.

> "Then they drew near to the village where they were going, and He indicated that He would have gone farther. But they constrained Him, saying, 'Abide with us, for it is toward evening, and the day is far spent.' And He went in to stay with them" (Luke 24:28-29).

Do you want a visitation from Jesus? Stay on the road of passion, as that's the key.

"Constrain" means "with a burning fervency, with a passion." They were saying, "No, no, no! Don't go!" Jesus agreed. When He broke bread and blessed them, their eyes were opened. Passion unlocks the door to intimacy and opens eyes.

When Paul was on the road to Emmaus, people say he was knocked off his horse. That's a metaphor, as He was on a high horse, proud, and arrogant. Paul wasn't on a horse, the glory of God knocked him to the ground.

A pastor once told me, "Nobody gets slain in the spirit. That's not in the Bible."

I said, "You'd better talk with Paul." Maybe the priests that were present when Solomon dedicated the temple would have some insight also. Unfortunately, some buy into a theological, doctrinal stance rather than the truth of the Word.

Paul went without sight for three days, which is prophetic. It's early in the morning of the third day, and our eyes are being opened! Luke 9:27 says, "I'll tell you of a truth. There are some of you standing here, they shall not taste of death until they see the Kingdom of God."

Peter, James, and John are the only three that taught on the "parousia," or the presencing of God together with us, and the "phanariot"—the open manifestation of God before the return of God. They were looking for that manifestation of visual capacity for the Church because they knew it would come just prior to the return of Jesus. Studying this will excite you because it's talking about this generation.

The word "see" is significant here. After studying this at length, something struck me: Being spiritually blind is the equivalent of physical blindness. For a Christian, being spiritually blind is more incapacitating than natural blindness because in John 5:19 Jesus said, "I only do what I see the Father doing."

"Then Jesus answered and said to them, 'Most assuredly, I say to you, the Son can do nothing of Himself, but what He sees the Father do; for whatever He does, the Son also does in like manner."

He's our pattern for life, and if Jesus has a visual capacity and can only do what He saw the Father doing, then we need to see! It's good news that He said, "What I can do, you can do."

"Most assuredly, I say to you, he who believes in Me, the works that I do he will do also; and greater works than these he will do, because I go to My Father" (John 14:12).

If we don't see, we can be hindered in our spiritual capacity and effectiveness in the Kingdom.

God, in His mercy and grace, has had a forerunner or remnant company of believers that walked in this visual capacity from the establishment of the Church until now. If you study history, they're called, "the mystic saints" or "the mystical saints." You are mystical! Some people don't like that word as they believe it's New Age.

No, it's not New Age! It's from Ages Old. If you don't believe you're mystical, explain the New Birth to me. You've already had a mystical experience that we can't define except that we translated from darkness to light. What does that look like? We don't want to be handicapped in the realm of the spirit by not exercising our spiritual senses.

"The God of our Lord Jesus Christ, the Father of Glory may give unto you the Spirit of wisdom and revelation and the knowledge of Him, that the eyes of your understanding being enlightened that you may know what is the hope of your calling and the richness of your inheritance in the saints" (Ephesians 1:17-19).

How do we learn to see into the Kingdom of God or the spirit realm? Many have experienced, seen, are engaging, and going, yet others are still thinking, "How do I break through?" That's okay! If you've already got a visual capacity and get an occasional glimpse, I hope and pray that's not enough for you. Remain consistently passionate for more of Him.

Your Imagination Is a Reality

Here's a key to seeing the unseen: Jesus considered imagination reality. In Matthew 5:28, He said: "Whoever looks on a woman to lust after her has committed adultery with her already in his heart." The one who did this would be judged and condemned for it, because to Jesus, this was reality.

Job 31:1 says: "I have made a covenant with my eyes." In this world in which we live, it's almost impossible to not be inundated and overwhelmed with visual images that can cause you to stumble. In America, with the many places a person could vacation, I don't understand Christians who like to go to Las Vegas where naked bodies are plastered on billboards, taxis, and everywhere you look. We've become hardened to it because these unclean things have become the norm in our society.

When Reshma and I got engaged, we waited nine months for her to get her fiancée visa. When she finally arrived at the airport in America, I told her, "You're going have to be my gauge, if you will, because I've lived in this nation far too long." She was coming from a country that had no open displays of sexuality.

THE EYES OF YOUR UNDERSTANDING ENLIGHTENED

As we were leaving the airport, I heard Reshma say, "Oh, no!" Seeing the lustful displays presented openly literally shocked her. That may sound funny to us, but it stained her righteous spirit and her purity. I, however, had been so hardened to it that after years of seeing it around me, it didn't affect me anymore.

I cried out, "Dear God, help!" Scripture says that living among those in Sodom and Gomorrah vexed righteous Lot's spirit. When we become hardened and desensitized to the purity of spirit to which we're called, we don't even recognize when we've lost it. Make a covenant with your eyes!

You look and can't help but see, but I submit to you that it's not your physical eyes that we're talking about—it's your spiritual eyes! When you see something inappropriate, you can push it away, but meditating on it will defile you. That's why 2 Corinthians 10:5 tells us to "Cast down imaginations":

> "Casting down imaginations, and every high thing that exalteth itself against the knowledge of God, and bringing into captivity every thought to the obedience of Christ" (KJV).

Rid yourself of the spiritual, visual things that will defile you. Cast it down or risk it becoming a reality for which you'll be judged. The majority of people have never understood that the imagination affects the course of your life and can hinder your walk with God.

When the Lord first started teaching me about guarding my eyes and thoughts, I realized that my imagination was undisciplined. Our imagination likes to go off on its own when we least expect it. The vast majority of us allow our imagination to go where it wants to go. We can't do that!

Our God is a creative God and has given us a creative ability. We're made in His image and His creative ability. Without disciplining that creative imagination, we defile or dishonor God. We must take authority.

I started the process by saying, "Lord, I'm going to take captive every thought and every imagination." It seemed that I dealt with this battle non-stop for days. Cast it down! Cast it down! Cast it down! But after a short time it was as if the devil said, "This isn't working anymore. We have to come up with a different strategy."

I trained myself to say, "No!" if something inappropriate came into my thoughts. This can be difficult when you're physically tired. In ministry and the prophetic, I try to avoid prophesying over people when I'm tired because it can be dangerous. When we have meetings around the world, it's our practice to arrive a couple of days early so we're rested, at our best, and don't cheat the people out of the ministry God desires to do.

What you see can affect what you think, and what you think can affect what you see, both naturally and spiritually. What you see in the natural can affect how you think and how you think can affect what you see in the realm of the spirit.

Matthew 12:36 says, "But I say unto you that for every idle word men may speak, they will give an account." That term, "word" is rhema and has tremendous implications. You will give an account for every idle, flippant comment about the revelation God gives you.

Matthew 12 continues: "For by your words you will be justified, and by your words you will be condemned." The term "word" here is logos (v 37) which includes your capacity for thought. By your thoughts you will be justified, and by your thoughts you will be condemned. I've seen and recognize scribe angels assigned to every human being, recording every thought, word, and action. You'll give account for all of it. The good news is that Jesus provided you a heavenly eraser called the blood of Jesus.

Two basic Greek words deal with the word "mind." In Matthew 22:37, Jesus said: "You shall love the Lord your God with all your heart, with all your soul, and with all your mind" (NASB).

The Greek word for heart is "dianoia." *The New Dictionary of Theology* says that when the Greek word "dianoia" is used in relation to the heart, it always means imagination. *Vine's Dictionary* says dianoia is the faculty renewed by the Holy Spirit called the imagination. Therefore, Matthew 22:37 is saying, "You shall love the Lord your God with all your heart, with all your soul, and with all of your imagination."

You love God with your imagination by properly framing pictures of the Kingdom in your imagination. For instance, when I pray, I choose to see Jesus. This is becoming easier because I can see Him now and have practiced doing so. When you pray, worship, and are in the Word, you focus on Him and see Jesus. That's loving God.

I'm an avid reader and have read thousands of books in my lifetime. As a kid, I loved science fiction. When you read a book, your imagination turns on and you see what's happening. Likewise, when you read the Bible, you're picturing it as you read. If you have the opportunity to travel to Israel, you can picture the Bible as it comes alive.

Enjoying your imagination is loving God. When you read about the road to Emmaus, for example, you shouldn't just read it in the third person as a story. When I read that passage, I see myself walking there.

My name, Bruce, is Cleopas, and it means "called of God." As I see Jesus approach, I start talking with Him. When worshipping

God, you may fall on your face in the natural, but you see yourself at His feet. As you focus on Jesus and practice this sanctified imagination, activation takes place and will take you to the destination.

In Luke 1:29, the second Greek word for "mind" is used. When Gabriel came to Mary, she was troubled at his saying: "But she was very perplexed at this statement, and kept pondering what kind of salutation this was" (NASB).

The word "pondering" is the Greek word "dialogismo," and it means the logical reasoning mind. Some have said, "Stop using your logic and reason and just go by the spirit." God gave you a mind to use, but there's a proper protocol, and you must sanctify it. I again emphasize what our stance should be:

"Father, all that I am, all that I ever hope to be, I submit to You. I submit my logical reasoning mind, my imagination, all my successes, and failures."

Sanctify your imagination by the blood of Jesus, and offer it as a living sacrifice (which are your members), which is your reasonable service. The Lord most often speaks in thoughts and impressions and through the still small voice in your heart. The problem is that because we're so undisciplined and haven't harnessed these gifts, we often don't recognize when God speaks. Most people think they're hearing themselves. I laugh and say, "You're not that smart!" It does, however, take time and practice to learn to discern the difference.

You have "dianoia"—the imagination—sanctified and "dialogismo"—the logical reasoning mind. Paul used the logical reasoning mind frequently. Acts 18:4 says, "And he reasoned in the synagogue every Sabbath, and persuaded both Jews and Greeks." That's good for Paul, as a Pharisee who knew his stuff, but most of us aren't there. However, God can give you wisdom if you lack wisdom.

THE EYES OF YOUR UNDERSTANDING ENLIGHTENED

Sanctify your imagination by the blood of Jesus, and offer it as a living sacrifice, which is your reasonable service.

Approximately 25 years ago, I was teaching in a meeting and talking about a particular Scripture. I said, "In the Greek it means …" and gave a definition. In my mind I thought, *What am I saying? I've never studied that.*

Afterwards I looked it up and got excited because the definition I had provided was exactly right. I asked the Lord, "Lord, what was that?"

He said, "I gave you wisdom."

Wow! I've done this with Rabbis, giving the Hebrew definition of words as I allowed God to bring me revelation rather than relying on my studies. Do I speak Hebrew? No! That's what it means to have the mind of Christ.

When I first got saved in the '80s, I was taught that we have the mind of Christ. One day, the Lord said to me, "Well, use it!" Sanctify your mind, take it out of that little jar on the shelf and use it.

Christians are often collectors. We collect prophecies, miracles, snippets of revelation, and then say, "Look at my collection!" but very few Christians walk it out and apply it to their life.

Who do you think wants you to misunderstand imagination? The devil, of course! Ephesians talks about the eyes of your understanding—dianoia—or imagination. Paul prayed that the eyes of your imagination would be enlightened. That means there's a connection between the part of your mind that sees images, pictures, and dreams, and the heart.

To doubt with the heart literally means to doubt with your imagination. For some years, the Lord released me to address this as I minister. When people ask me to pray for healing, I do a simple test. After they share their physical ailment, I ask, "How are you going to know you're healed?"

Some will ask, "What do you mean?" Others say they've come forward "by faith."

My next question is, "What does faith look like? What do you believe? What is your faith creating?"

If they say something like, "Well, I've got this horrible pain, I guess faith looks like having no more pain." Very seldom does God direct me to pray for them. Instead, I say, "I agree with you. Now move!"

"The pain is gone!" they often exclaim. Why? Because they saw themselves healed. That revelation changed the ministry overnight.

I share a funny testimony in many places because of the reaction I see in recipients. While ministering in Belfast, Northern Ireland, a woman came up for prayer. I asked her, "What do you need from the Lord?"

"I have a heart condition," she said. "I want a new heart. I don't want a refit heart. I want a new heart."

Before I could even ask her any questions, I suddenly noticed an angel come through the backdoor of the church carrying a platter with a beating heart. I glanced at this scene, then brought my attention back to her. Seeing me look, she looked, too. Her eyes widened, then she closed them tight.

"You saw him, too!" I said, laughing. When the angel walked up between us, I stepped back. He looked at me, nodded, picked up the heart from the platter, then reached into her chest and placed the new heart there.

As I watched him put his hand into her chest, she said, "Ahh!" Then the angel reached further down. Though she hadn't told me about other issues, the Lord knew what she needed. The angel made an adjustment in her, then held his hand out, looked at me and left.

"I guess we don't have to pray," I said to her. "You're healed. We're just going to agree with what we saw the Father doing."

She returned home that night and threw out her heart medication. I didn't tell her to do that because there can be withdrawal symptoms when medication is stopped suddenly, which can be very dangerous. That evening, she cooked and ate a spicy, greasy meal that she hadn't been able to eat in years. She slept soundly for the first time since her heart diagnosis nine years earlier.

When she saw her doctor a month later for her regular checkup, he said, "Wow! Your heart is like the heart of a 20-year-old. What have you been doing?"

"Well, this angel came and..." she explained.

"Whatever you're doing," her doctor said, "just keep doing it!"

She saw and she received! Witnessing these encounters makes ministry really exciting! If you can somehow challenge people not only to hope in faith, but to believe and see it by faith, nine out of ten receive healing. We practice this all over the world, and it's been amazing to witness!

In 1 Kings 17, my favorite prophet, Elijah, prophesied no rain. In 1 Kings 18, he says, "Tell Ahab I'm here. There's going to be rain." Then he says, "I challenge you to come up to Mt. Carmel. The God who answers by fire, He is God." If you know the story, he killed 450 false prophets. He had them outnumbered because one put a thousand to flight (Deuteronomy 32:30).

Elijah then went to the top of the mountain and upon hearing of a small cloud, said, "I hear the sound of the abundance of rain. Go tell Ahab, 'Here it comes!'"

The next day, after Ahab ran home and whined to Jezebel, Jezebel sent out a messenger. Messengers were very athletic because they were runners, so here's this skinny, little messenger who says to Elijah, "Here's the message: See if I don't do to you about this time tomorrow what you have done to all my prophets."

Scripture says, "When Elijah saw, he ran." What did he see? The skinny little runt messenger? No! Elijah had just killed 450 false prophets! Was it the parchment he saw? No! He saw (in his imagination) his head being removed, and when it became a reality in his imagination, he ran. When you ask for prayer, see the answers and you'll receive. That's the sanctified imagination.

When You Pray, See it!

In the '80s, my dad's friend, Smitty, was preaching in an open field meeting. From the platform he preached, "Jesus can do anything! He can heal anything!"

"Anything?" a lady in the crowd yelled.

"Absolutely!" he said.

Pulling back the rope around the stage area, she entered the platform area. In a wheelchair, she pulled the blanket off her legs, revealing that she had no legs.

"Can He heal this?" she asked.

"Absolutely!" Smitty said with unwavering confidence.

"Fine," she said.

Pushing herself off the wheelchair, two legs instantly appeared before she hit the ground.

Later, Smitty said, "She had no faith but was prodding and provoking me. When I said, 'Absolutely!' I saw legs in the spirit." His faith went—poof—and when she stood up, she had legs!

Oftentimes, the evangelist says, "Well, if you just had faith, you'd have been healed." I hate that, as they're blaming their lack of faith on somebody else. Why not simply tell them the truth? Sometimes, however, that statement is accurate.

When I was younger, I became so frustrated that I approached the evangelist. "Brother," I said. "How much faith did Lazarus have? Where's your faith? Lazarus was dead, in case you don't know!" Then I left.

God's Word says, "You are healed," so if you see yourself as sick, you'll be sick. If you see yourself healed, you'll be healed! When you pray, see it, and you'll find answers to prayers speedily because imagination is reality. The heart makes contact with the spirit realm and the mouth releases the power of that realm.

The eyes of our imagination should be enlightened—by the Holy Spirit. The word "enlightened" is the Greek word "photizo," which is where we get the word photograph. We could paraphrase and put it together like this:

Paul was praying that the eyes of our imagination might receive pictures of the Kingdom of heaven so that we might know our destiny.

Photizo. Dianoia and photizo. Your imagination is designed to receive pictures so you might know your destiny. The Lord brought me to where I am today because of this principle. When I was born again, I knew I had a call of God on my life but was very shy and scared to death of people. In preaching class at Bible College, I chose to fail instead of doing the class, yet I couldn't get away from the call on my life or the burning passion in my heart.

A friend at school was working his way through college by working as the night guard on campus. When I convinced him to let me into the school campus chapel at night, he said, "Just don't turn anything on because I'll get in trouble."

"Okay," I agreed. So, every night at 9 o'clock, I'd have a church service. I'd go to the chapel, then lay out my Bible on the podium to preach. I preached and preached!

About three months later, another friend heard what I had been doing and said, "Can I come and lead worship?"

"Sure!" I said. "I guess every service needs worship." He led worship and then I preached to an empty room. Knowing I had a destiny, I'd envision people in the seats and kept practicing.

After six months, my spiritual eyes were opened, and I saw the room filled with angels! "Wow!" I marveled. I kept preaching because angels know how to say "Amen!" It was the best service I'd ever experienced. The message wasn't that great, but God was doing something as I focused and practiced. That which I focused on, I connected with, and that which I connected with brought activation.

Because I kept practicing throughout my life, whenever I was asked to share somewhere, I'd always agree. Later, I'd slap myself thinking, *What am I doing?* because I was still terrified of speaking. I knew I was doing all right because my knees were applauding! I shook so badly that you could hear my knees knocking together! Yet I forced myself to stand up there because I kept seeing what God had shown me.

Finally, the breakthrough came and the ministry I walk in today is the fulfillment of that breakthrough. My God-given destiny became my reality because I focused on the promise, not on the situation. I could still be working some nine-to-five, dead-end job somewhere if I hadn't dared to believe. Instead, I kept seeing my destiny because the eyes of my imagination were receiving pictures of the Kingdom of God out of the book of my destiny.

Sanctified Imagination, the Bridge between Soul and Spirit

The bridge between the soul and the spirit is the bridge of a sanctified imagination. Jesus considered this a reality.

> "This book of the law shall not depart out of thy mouth; but thou shalt meditate therein day and night, that thou mayest observe to do according to all that is written therein: for then thou shalt make thy way prosperous, and then thou shalt have good success" (Joshua 1:8, KJV).

The word "meditate" means "imagine." It's a primitive root. "Hagah" or "doga" in the Hebrew means to murmur, and by implication means to ponder or to imagine. I mentioned earlier that in the natural, my childhood passion was to be a pilot and an astronaut. I had posters of the Cessna 150, Cessna 2T and posters of the cockpit in my bedroom, so I knew exactly where the instruments were. I'd imagine my dreams regularly because I read a lot about flying and knew what it would feel like.

When I was a bit older, I had an opportunity to go to the airfield, get in an airplane and go for a test ride because I was going to take lessons. In a test ride, they take you up to a certain altitude and then say, "Okay, take the controls." Either they have great faith or they're insane!

After the instructor told me to take the controls, he said, "Bank left."

As he watched me follow his instruction, he asked, "How many hours have you got?"

"I've never been in an airplane before," I said.

"Yes, you have," he insisted. "How many hours have you got behind you?"

"None," I assured him.

"Boy! You must be a natural then!"

I wasn't a natural, but I had seen it for years in my imagination!

The same scenario happened when I got into a helicopter. They asked, "How many hours have you got?"

"I've never done this before," I'd say.

They couldn't believe it. That which I had envisioned for years had become a reality. This is on a lesser, natural level, but is still truth. There's power in a sanctified imagination and it reflects in your reality.

> "Let no man despise your youth. Be an example for the believers in word, in conversation, in love, in spirit, in faith, and in purity till I come. Till I come, give attendance to reading, to exhortation, to doctrine. Neglect not the gift that is in you, which was given you by prophecy, with the laying on of the hands of the presbytery" (1 Timothy 4:12-14, AKJV).

In other words, meditate upon these things. Imagine them and see them as reality. If you received a prophetic word that you're going to go to the nations to preach the Gospel, see it and meditate on it. Repeat it, read it, and see it. Repeat it, read it, and see it. Doing this honors God. Where most Christians fall down is after receiving a prophetic word, they write it out, but then say, "Great! Next? Got another word for me?"

If you received a prophetic word that you're going to go to the nations to preach the Gospel, see it and meditate on it. Repeat it, read it, and see it.

We've watched this dynamic happen all over the world. The Lord doesn't allow me to give prophetic words very often anymore because people have become dependent upon the gift and not upon God. When they say to me, "Got a word for me?" I grab the Bible and tell them, "Yes! Here's your Word from the Lord. Walk in it!" We must stop creating a culture of problem-fed Christians and help them grow up.

God gave you an imagination for you to use. Everything that surrounds us every day was created by somebody's imagination. A picture or a thought stirred in someone, they mulled it over as it took clarity, then it dropped into the heart and came forth as a reality.

One day, while preaching at a church in Seattle, everything stopped suddenly. Looking around, I asked myself, *What's going on?* In that moment, everything throughout history rolled up like a scroll. Seeing back to the beginning, I saw all of creation go into the Father's mouth, set into His heart, and up into His imagination. Knowing this was of God, I watched as He released this to me—seeing God create in His imagination and drop it into his heart; then out of the abundance of His heart, He spoke and all of creation unfurled up to the current time again. Seeing this in my spirit almost knocked me over!

God was dealing with me about what I was teaching regarding sin. Thoughts are not sin, but meditating on those thoughts becomes sin. The devil operates through thoughts. The moment God gives you a promise, the devil throws doubt at you. The moment you make a mistake, he speaks condemnation. If you meditate on the mistake, it drops into your heart, and out of the abundance of the heart it's released.

I've seen many people in the natural, by the eyes of my spirit, with terrible bruising around their mouth as they've agreed with the devil's curses over them. Making vows and curses after believing the enemy's lies bruises their spiritual mouth.

> "And the LORD said, Behold, the people is one, and they have all one language; and this they begin to do: and now nothing will be restrained from them, which they have imagined to do" (Genesis 11:6, KJV).

That's a powerful word! Individually and corporately, if an individual or corporate body shares the same vision, and then speaks in accordance with that vision, nothing is im-possible. It starts with the imagination.

Imagine for a moment that instead of buying an airline ticket, you see yourself owning the airline. A friend of mine had been told that God was going to start giving him prophetic ability to speak into the lives of businessmen and businesswomen. Not only that, the Lord would give him properties to use for the Kingdom.

This brother was called to Peru to minister, where a business owner had built a 5-star resort hotel that was losing money left and right. Because the business owner knew of his prophetic gift, he asked for his help. "Would you please come and pray and tell me what the Lord says about why this is happening to my hotel?"

My friend went to the hotel and said, "I'm just going to walk around for a while." He walked throughout the offices, praying as he went. A couple of hours later, he came into the owner's office and said, "The Lord showed me what's going on."

"What?" He asked.

"Well, this person in finance is stealing," and then he identified others who were stealing from him. He went down the list of the people robbing him blind within his own organization.

He told the owner, "It's bad, but the worst part is that you didn't vet any of these people or discern who they were when you hired them."

"You're right," the businessman admitted. "I hired a headhunter that filled the positions."

The man fired every employee that had stolen from him. Then he told my friend, "You know what? You give me one dollar, and I'm going to give you this hotel for your ministry." With a brand new 5-star resort hotel for ministry, one could have a Bible school or conference center! The possibilities are endless. Think big and imagine big as God is a big God!

How did Moses survive 40 years in the wilderness? 40 years in Egypt, in the lap of luxury, he lived in the courts of the pharaoh. He had untold wealth and riches but knew he had a destiny. He tried to help God by making it happen but ran into the wilderness, and for 40 years, he tended sheep on the backside of the desert.

He finally arrived at Mt. Horeb, which means desolation and despair, where he was broken. In that place of brokenness, at the end of his flesh, he died to himself and saw something he'd never seen before. He learned a key lesson about crucifying the flesh.

Seeing a bush engulfed in flames yet not consumed, he walked up to the bush and heard the voice say, "Moses, Moses!" An angel in the burning bush spoke twice. "Take the sandals off your feet."

As he obeyed, he entered into a sandal covenant with God: His Inheritance.

> "By Faith, Moses forsook Egypt, not fearing the wrath of the king, for he endured as seeing Him who is invisible" (Hebrews 11:27, KJV).

Moses endured by seeing Him who is invisible. First the burning bush was in his mind, then a pillar of fire and a pillar of cloud, then the glory of God on Mt. Sinai, and lastly, a face-to-face encounter. His ability to see progressed, leading him to a life-long face-to-face encounter of knowing God.

Seeing in the spirit starts with a sanctified imagination that becomes the bridge that carries you deeper into the things of the spirit. Moses came to the end of his life and was in perfect health. At 120 years old, he had the strength of a young man. When God said, "Your job is done," he died, not because he was feeble and ill. His body didn't decay at the normal human rate because he had spent so much time in the manifest presence of the living God. Like Moses was irradiated with glory and life, this generation is called to know Him face to face, to go from glory to glory not sickness to sickness, or decay to decay.

Isaiah 26:3 says: "You will keep Him in perfect peace whose mind is fixed on you." The word "mind" is the Greek word "fiatzo" which means "imagination." When you pray, see Him. When you talk to Him, see Him. When you invite Him, see Him. Many people try this and say, "What does He look like? Is my image of Him accurate?" Who cares! Take a step of faith and don't worry about accuracy. Just move forward!

While we were in Shanghai, some said, "Is it okay if God is Chinese?"

THE EYES OF YOUR UNDERSTANDING ENLIGHTENED

When you pray, see Him. When you talk to Him, see Him. When you invite Him, see Him.

"Absolutely!" I said.

"Really?" they asked.

"Aren't we created in His image?" I asked.

Don't get hung up on those details because when you're focusing, focus brings connection, and when connection comes, clarity comes and those questions disappear.

Practice, as practice makes you proficient. I've told you about Brother Buetler meeting with Jesus, so you know the principles. As I put this into practice, it became my reality and enabled me to now see Jesus regularly.

Your spirit is like a tuner on an FM radio dial. We could be talking about natural things, then start talking about the Lord, which switches the dial to another frequency. If I'm doing other things, then start talking about the things of the spirit, my spiritual eyes engage. Sometimes I'm not necessarily thinking about the things of the Kingdom, but I know He's there because I can sense Him, feel him, and sometimes hear Him.

Once Reshma and another female pastor were on a road trip traveling to Alaska to minister, and I was headed another direction from Seattle. I asked the Lord, "Lord, do You want to go on a road trip?"

"Yeah!" He said.

When we got in the car, I didn't see the door open but heard it open and close as He sat down in the passenger's seat. I saw

Him clearly, dressed in white robes. We drove along, talking and enjoying a great time together as He's my best friend and we share fellowship.

We came into the area where Microsoft, Amazon, Starbucks, and other prestigious companies are located. With obviously a lot of money in the area, we saw high-end sports cars around us. Seeing the beautiful Mercedes, Audis, BMWs, Rolls Royces, Jaguars, Ferraris, and Bentleys, I asked the Lord, "Hey, Lord, what kind of car do You like?"

With a twinkle in His eyes, He said, "BMW."

"BMW? Really?"

He laughed and said, "Be My Witness!" It was fun! I share that story as someone once bought a BMW and put a "Be My Witness" tag on it. This is how real and tangible this is. It makes walking with God an adventure. It starts with a sanctified imagination and then focusing and paying the price needed to focus.

Take the principles presented here and make them your own. Passionate focus releases purposeful pursuit, which releases intimacy that will change your life. God can manifest His presence in any way He chooses. I remember in Bible College they said, "How many angels can stand on the head of a pin?"

Hearing that, I'd think, *You've got to be kidding me. What Bible College did I get into? Stand on the head of a pin!*

I said, "As many as He wants. He's God!"

They'd respond, "You're no fun!"

As we conduct the schools across the world, the Lord often manifests His presence among us and visits us. Reshma and I have watched Jesus do this often. He's real.

Practice!

Practice using your sanctified imagination. See yourself walking through your home, but invite Jesus to walk with you. See Him walking with you—listen to Him, watch what He does and you'll be astonished. That's your homework.

Putting these principles into practice will revolutionize your walk with God. It drastically changed my life and the lives of countless others. I'm not taking experiences and making them on par with Scripture but instead taking Scripture and unlocking experience. Let's go a bit further:

> "Looking unto Jesus the author and finisher of our faith; who for the joy that was set before him endured the cross, despising the shame, and is set down at the right hand of the throne of God" (Hebrews 12:2, KJV).

Draw near to God and He will draw near to you. Sometimes this happens sovereignly, but He's commanding us to do this in this hour. He made a way for us to come before the throne of God by setting our hearts and imagination on the Lord. When Peter walked on the water, the first thing he had to do was get out of the boat. The first thing you've got to do is to step out of your boat of doubt and unbelief and take a step of faith.

I used to practice walking on water—not the frozen kind. I'd step off the boat I was on and simply practice walking on water. I learned to swim really well, but it didn't discourage me because I believe in practicing and acting by faith.

I remember learning about prophecy at age 15, and as mentioned earlier, I was shy. I'd see people with the gift of tongues and interpretation of tongues, and once in a while when somebody gave a straight prophetic word, I liked it because it bypassed the middleman. Feeling a stirring inside, I thought, *Wow! I had too much coffee this morning because I'm getting the jitters.* I didn't know what was happening.

For a time I would think, *Maybe I've got a word,* and I would give two, three, or four words, or maybe even a sentence. *Whew!* I thought. Thank God I did it! Afraid of making a mistake and looking even more foolish to everybody, I had fear of man. This continued for two or three years and created a dynamic where sometimes I was obedient, and sometimes I wasn't obedient.

God, in His mercy and grace, was teaching me to know His voice. He never gave me a prophetic voice like some people who get a scroll with the words written on it. The most I got was a nudge, and unless I opened my mouth, I wouldn't know what it was. After much practice and stepping out in faith I became more proficient, but after a few years, my confidence in God's ability developed the gift of prophecy.

When people know you hear God's voice and can prophesy, they often seek you out for a prophetic word. The danger can come when you want to look good in front of people and feel a "need" to deliver something. With the pressure of man, suddenly you can be "prophelying" and prophesy to the idols in people's hearts.

The mantle of a prophet enables a person to read people's mail, but that's not what you're called to do! The danger and error come when people are known for their prophetic words and are expected to prophesy every day.

Take a step of faith. You might make a mistake or may think, *Is this me or is it God?* Err on the side of faith and say, "Lord, I trust You. You're going to correct me if I'm wrong." Keep going, continue journaling, and soon you'll realize you're walking in it.

THE EYES OF YOUR UNDERSTANDING ENLIGHTENED

As you develop confidence, opportunities will break open for you to engage with God face to face. The first time I was before the throne of God was as tangible as the natural realm. That's an insufficient description because once you've seen heaven and seen God, everything in this earth seems dull.

I used to love to travel and see the great wonders and beautiful sites around the world. I'm not a tourist anymore as my interest has waned after seeing God's wonders in the spiritual realm. Nothing compares!

I can't do justice in describing my first time before the throne of God. The throne was 200 thousand miles high and 200 thousand miles wide. The Father, seated on the throne, said, "Look to the right," so I looked to the right.

With supernatural vision in heaven, one can see for a million miles both ways, filled with mansions. It's Paradise and it's real!

It all started with a hope, glimpse, and glimmer from Scripture that fanned the flame of passion. That passion became a desire that pushed me beyond where faith will fail, because I wouldn't quit. God then unlocked scriptural precedents into tools that I passionately activated and pursued, because practice makes proficient. I kept going—and going and going—until breakthrough came. I'm giving you tools I received on that journey, which are effective only if you use them.

Let me give you an example. Have you ever ridden a horse or seen someone ride a horse? They use a saddle, a bridle, and a

Once you've seen heaven and seen God, everything in this earth seems dull.

harness, right? Because of our natural understanding of what is necessary to ride a horse, we have a "picture" to draw upon when we begin the process of imagining and focusing. That's a picture we can "see."

I've always imagined that when Jesus comes back on a white horse with the host of heaven, there would be chariots and horses with harnesses and bridles, until one day, I had an encounter with a chariot of fire and the heavenly beings that looked like horses. When they came into the auditorium by the spirit, it was immediately evident to me via the revelation of the Holy Spirit that these beings had great intelligence, tremendous love, and compassion. Their ability to communicate was clear as I "heard" one of them communicating with me in my spirit. It communicated with my heart and soul, saying, "These are not necessary." Immediately the bridle and harness vanished! He then communicated in that same manner, "the bond is love." This should help you in your understanding of how focus, connection, and activation work. We start by focusing on an image in our imagination. When the connection comes, (in this case a heavenly encounter) it brings an activation of greater clarity. The presumptive aspects of that imagination are clarified by the interaction with the reality of that realm.

My presumption based on my culture, environment and life experiences framed an image, even during an encounter, of what was normal to me. But as I continued to engage, revelation and clarity came.

Sanctify your imagination daily. Every morning, pray, "Father, I sanctify this and give it to You." If you're in business, you'll discover that God will give you creative ideas. If you're in ministry, God will give you tremendous revelation, insight, and creative ways to communicate with a logical reasoning mind. The natural mind works at 1% capacity, compared to the Kingdom of heaven, which is without limit.

My Dad had a ministry in Seattle, Washington, and as I developed in my calling, we started a church. On Monday nights, we'd have what we called a Holy Spirit night, which was open to anybody. We had no agenda and allowed the Holy Ghost to lead. The Holy Ghost would give either Dad or me a message, so even though we'd come prepared, we always yielded to Him. 200-300 people came from Canada and other states of the US. We paired off to pray for each other because that brought activation, and we wanted to train and equip them.

My dad had gone to sit in the back by a woman who was sitting alone. "Who brought you?" He asked. "You're a guest I haven't seen before."

Dad sensed something in the spirit and asked, "Do you need deliverance?"

"Well," she replied, "my pastor's wife doesn't think so."

"Okay," Dad said.

Suddenly, she got up. Although quite small, a thought went through my dad's head: *If I don't get up, she's going to kick me, and I don't want to be kicked!*

He started to get up and said to the demon in the woman, "Come out!" She manifested and sat on top of him. At this point, Dad lost all ministry etiquette that he'd learned, even while ministering with Lester Sumrall!

While I stood at the front talking to somebody, I heard, "Come out! Come out!" There were about 40 rows of chairs in front, and though I saw the chairs parting, nobody was there. This demonized woman was dragging my dad along on the ground.

I said, "Excuse me."

Seeing that she had dragged Dad from the back of the building to the second row from the front, I prayed, "Lord, what do You say…"

Immediately I saw the anointing of God flow and the demonic stronghold break.

The Lord said, "Release the anointing."

"I release the anointing in the Name of Jesus," I declared.

Immediately the demon left, then Dad pulled himself up and asked, "Who brought this woman? Get her saved and filled with the Holy Spirit!"

"Lord, what was that all about?" I prayed.

The Lord said, "If you learn to see, ministry is easy."

Chapter Nine

THE REVELATION OF LIGHT

KETUBAH is the Hebrew word for "marriage covenant." "Khatan" is the Hebrew word for the bridegroom. In our covenant with the Lord, He is the Bridegroom. Khatan also means, "one who joins himself," so another name for God is "He who joins Himself." This revelation will change your life.

Once we've accepted the Lord, and He becomes our Bridegroom, He joins Himself to us. A joining is not merely coming alongside. A joining is a "fusing together with." That's how you become one new creation, because there's a new reality and a new understanding. You're no longer thinking, *I'm here and Jesus is there.* You become one new creation, joining together with Him. This is why Scripture speaks of the mystery of the husband and wife because we don't fully comprehend the joining and becoming one. In Scripture, the Bridegroom is He who joins.

The loved one becomes one with you, not just with your good characteristics. He joins together with you in your darkness, in the evil, the mistakes, and flaws within you. If you understand the heart of the Bridegroom, He takes those things upon Himself so that you are no longer what you once were. If He joins Himself to us and we're fused together with Him, it makes more sense when we speak of "where He is, there we are also" or "I will never leave you nor forsake you" or "He loves you with an unfathomable love." He's fused Himself together with you, and in this process, as you yield to the love of the Bridegroom, you become something new in Him.

You may wonder what this has to do with translation. He does the translation. Not you. You're so entwined together with the Lord that you could never be separated no matter how dark or joyful the days. When we walk together with Him, everything changes.

Jesus speaks of the importance of being equally yoked. He's speaking of Himself, the Bridegroom and the Bride. The two must become one in purpose, one in heart, one in vision and in focus.

As Christians, if we're trying to pull this way to do our own thing, when He's saying, "No, let's go this way," how far do you think you'll get? That yoke is not going to function. But when you know He's fused with you, the rest becomes easy. Relationship becomes easy, and fellowship becomes easy because He's not far off out there, He's here right now. In those quiet moments, as you listen, He speaks and whispers into your ear.

Remember when Elijah ran from Jezebel and lay under the juniper tree wanting to die? The angel fed him twice and he continued on to Mt. Horeb, meaning the place of desolation and despair. In a cave, he faced a mountain of desolation and despair that was crushing him. When an earthquake came, God wasn't in the earthquake. A wind came, but God wasn't in the wind. A fire came, but God wasn't in the fire. Then came the still small voice, which speaks of intimacy. The still small voice was God. He longs for intimacy and speaks through intimacy.

THE REVELATION OF LIGHT

When you become aware of the fusion you have with Him, you can hear the slightest whisper in that place of intimacy like two lovers lying on the same pillow whispering in each other's ear.

I'm attempting to release your understanding so you can grasp this truth and walk in it. I can give you principles, share testimonies or examples, but ultimately, this is between you and the Lord. As you learn that you're fused together with Him in this place of intimacy, it changes everything! You'll be saying, "I can't fail!" You may make mistakes but you can't fail as you confess those things to Him and let Him heal and carry you.

As you grow in this revelation, listen to Him and do what He says. You can't fail. Grasp this truth as imperative for the days ahead. Read Song of Solomon 5:10-6:2. I also like Song of Solomon Chapter 8, which says, "Who is this that comes out of the wilderness leaning upon her beloved?" The tests and trials in your life will cause you to depend on Him. You lean upon Him—as you come out of the wilderness experiences and fuse together with Him!

Isaiah 60:1-3 is one of my favorite, but most misunderstood and compelling revelations about translation, or walking in the realm of the spirit:

"Arise, shine; For your light has come! And the glory of the Lord is risen upon you. For behold, the darkness shall

As you learn that you're fused together with Him in this place of intimacy, it changes everything! You'll be saying, "I can't fail!"

cover the earth, And deep darkness the people; But the Lord will arise over you, And His glory will be seen upon you. The Gentiles shall come to your light, And kings to the brightness of your rising."

This is the year and the season to arise and shine; for your light has come and the glory of the Lord is risen upon you!

In July of 2013, I had just finished a conference in Maryland and Washington and was ready to return home. Reshma wasn't able to travel with me at that time as she was caring for our grandson at home. A pastor from our ministry alliance network called and said, "We're dedicating the church and ordaining people, and we want you to come."

This church was only 10-15 miles away, but I told him, "No, I'm tired. I want to go home."

"No!" he said. "We really want you to come and speak."

"You brought in international speakers, so you don't need me to come," I said. "I'm tired and I want to go home."

Then the Lord spoke to me. "Be quiet and say, 'Yes.'"

In obedience, I said, "Okay. What do you want me to do?"

"We want you to speak on the first night," he said.

I wasn't comfortable with that and told him "No, you've got Brother so and so from such and such, so it's covered."

"No," he responded. "He also wants you to speak."

"But that's his night," I said. "Why do you want me?"

Then the Lord said, "Be quiet and say, 'Yes.'"

I said, "Okay. What's the plan?"

"We're going to give you 15 minutes because you bring the glory."

15 minutes…? To bring the glory…? I thought. "Okay." I said, then went to the hotel and started praying.

"Lord," I prayed, "what is this about? They're saying, 'You bring the glory. You've got 15 minutes.' I have no idea what they're talking about. What do they mean 'I bring the glory?' That's not even a concept to me."

Immediately, I was in the spirit. As I stood, the Lord said, "Remove that garment."

As I tried to remove the garment by pulling it apart and off, a bright light shone. Startled, I dropped my hand and froze. I didn't know what to do.

Again, He said, "Remove the garment."

I took it off this time and stood as a being of light. Looking at myself again, I saw that I was clothed with a white garment and was wearing sandals of light. Looking behind me, I saw my flesh lying out as an old, used rag deflated on the ground.

In awe, I said, "Lord, what is this?"

He said, "Communicate to My people: It is time for them to move back toward the truth of who they are. They are light because they are created in My image, and they must comport themselves and carry themselves, to understand who they truly are." Then the vision ended.

I sat there, processing what had just happened. I'd never seen nor experienced anything like this before and was in the process of coming to grips with it. When we have experiences in God like this, we must jealously guard it. If we don't guard our experiences with God, time can pass and dim what we saw, then doubt creeps in. The devil will try to steal God encounters from you.

I said, "Father, forgive me. I need a confirmation on this."

I had a new Bible at that time. I don't normally open the Bible randomly and say, "Lord, speak." But this time however, I did just that. As I opened the Bible, it immediately fell open at Mark 9, the Mountain of Transfiguration.

The Father said, "You can do this by faith."

I closed the Bible and said, "Wow!"

I meditated on the passage of Scripture, then said, "Father, forgive me. Just one more confirmation."

This time I opened the Bible to 1 Timothy 1:7 that says, "I have not given you a spirit of fear but of power, love, and a sound mind."

"This is my grace," the Lord said. "Go and do it."

Closing the Bible, I said, "Yes, sir."

I began to pray that afternoon because the meeting was that night. "Father," I prayed, "what do You want me to share?"

"Share what I just shared with you," He said.

At the meeting that night, congressmen, senators, mayors, and other officials—believers and unbelievers—were present to dedicate this new building and to acknowledge what God was doing there.

The international speakers and the pastor came up to the stage as worship ended. The pastor reminded me, "Now, you've got 15 minutes. We've got a program we need to follow."

"Fine," I said.

The pastor handed me the microphone and I shared the experience the Lord had given me earlier. It took only nine minutes as I watched the clock. When I finished, the tangible power and presence of God had so saturated the atmosphere that nobody could move, leaving all in awe of God's manifested presence. The

THE REVELATION OF LIGHT

unsaved people's eyes widened, and Christians said, "What is this? What did he say?"

The pastor approached me and whispered, "Whatever He tells you to do, do it."

"I did," I said, and handed him the microphone. Bless his heart, because we're all trained this way; he didn't know what to do with the presence of God. When God's manifested presence comes, we must yield to it! Whatever He says, wait until He directs you to move! The pastor didn't understand that, so he jumped back into the program and the presence of God lifted.

When we talked about it afterwards, the pastor repented. He understood, but didn't know how to steward God's presence, as most people don't. We all learned a lesson that night.

The Lord said, "If you're obedient to Me, I can do more in a moment than you could do in a lifetime. You could have prayed, fasted, interceded, and done all the religious protocols you've learned to do—which are not bad—but if you'll allow My presence to come, you don't have to do all of that."

We respond to the leading of the Spirit. The Lord said, "As you learn to walk according to your first domain, that you are light, you'll learn to walk in this, and it will become normal."

In August of that year, we conducted a conference with Brother Sadhu Sundar Selvaraj as speaker. His stories are fascinating! We'd sit down before the meeting and I'd ask, "Who visited you last night? What was the Lord saying?"

"Abraham visited me last night," he said once, and then shared what Abraham said. "Just as Abraham was leaving, he turned around and said, 'Tell Bruce to study light because in it, he'll find the answers he's seeking.'" Sadhu had no knowledge of my experience concerning light in July, a month earlier. When I told Reshma what had happened, we were both filled with joy about what God was doing in our midst.

In September, we traveled to Sydney, Australia, to do a conference with brother Neville Johnson and brother Sadhu. In the hotel room I prayed, telling God, "You better give me something to share, otherwise…" when suddenly I was caught away in the spirit in a cave somewhere on the earth.

As a child, I loved National Geographic Magazine before the Discovery Channel existed. I could see the sun outside the cave entrance setting like a massive red ball going down in the Serengeti Desert. As I beheld this beautiful and powerful sun setting, I knew it spoke of the end of the age. In this cave, I was hidden in the cleft of the Rock—Jesus.

While I gazed at this wonder, Elijah suddenly appeared beside me. "Sir," I said, "why are you here?"

"The Lord sent me here," he replied. "He sent me to teach you how a man can go from this realm to the eternal realm without tasting death." He had my undivided attention because he did exactly that in Scripture!

Fascinated, I said, "Wow! What does this look like?"

He said, "Do what I do."

Extending his hand, it became light. As I tried to do the same, I forgot everything the Lord had taught me about light and was grunting, groaning, and struggling until Elijah started laughing at me.

"Remember what the Lord told you," he said. "This comes from rest and the fusing together. Just be hidden in Him. Rest!"

As I followed his words, I turned into light!

"Keep practicing," he said, so I kept practicing.

After some time, he said, "Good."

Standing in front of me, he held a key made of light. It was the same key God had given me some time ago. Instructing me, he said, "Put out your hand."

My hand was light, so as he set the key in my hand, it dissolved into me. Shocked, I said, "What did you do? What is that?"

"You are the key. You are the key. Light is the key that unlocks the door. You are light."

I was still trying to grasp his words when he said, "Follow me," and walked through the wall. When he walked through the wall, my focus was still on the key, and as I turned and followed him, I walked into the wall. That hurt!

I fell down as he laughed again. I thought, *What in the world are you doing?*

He said, "Remember what the Lord has taught you."

I sat there, meditating on the revelations the Lord had taught me about light, which took me to a place of peace and rest where I recognized who I am in Christ. Then I walked through the wall!

From July through September I focused my attention on studying light and practiced what God was teaching me as He established His Word by two or three witnesses. Envisioning myself divesting that garment of flesh and putting on the garment of light is my daily practice now.

When December arrived, I prayed, "Father, what are You saying for the New Year?"

He gave me Isaiah 60: "Arise, shine, for your light has come and the glory of the Lord is risen upon you." There's a direct correlation between recognizing that you're light and God's glory coming upon you.

Revelation Is Light

Back in the '70s when the faith movement was in full swing, they began to teach people to confess and memorize the Word. "Here are all the scriptures on healing. Here are all the scriptures on prosperity. Here's all the Scripture on…" It became a ritualistic formula people followed. We memorized a lot of Scripture!

God's Word is always effective. The application of the Word is where we can fail because it can become manipulation when we develop a religious practice and miss the personal relationship with God.

We must be a people of the Word. When light comes, revelation is released. Another word for revelation in Scripture is light. "For your light has come and the glory of the Lord is risen upon you" (Isaiah 60:1). Jesus is the Light of the World. And that Light came and it shone into great darkness. That was the revelation of the Messiah! Light and revelation work hand in hand and are fused together. You can't have one without the other.

Now you have a revelation of your true identity in Christ, and God's glory has a resting place in which it can be released through you. You can do nothing in Scripture without revelation. You can't even get saved without a revelation of your need for God! Revelation is where God breathes light, understanding, or insight into Scripture and it becomes tangible and real to you. From that point on you walk in it because that's who you are now. It's a release of His essence into you, which becomes a part of your character.

Season of Unparalleled Revelation Being Released

At the end of the age, "Arise and shine for your light has come" means that this is the season of the release of unparalleled revelation because in knowing Him we become like Him. He's

Revelation has come! The transforming understanding of your identity in Christ is necessary for you to shine like Jesus on the Mount of Transfiguration.

coming back for a Church without spot or blemish. He's doing a quick work at the end of the age, and if God doesn't intervene in the affairs of the Church, it will never happen because of the frailty of human flesh and our utter laziness and lack of passion for God.

Because He's fused Himself together with us as the Bridegroom and because He's taken on even our failings, we're positioned to receive His grace to receive the reality of Isaiah 60: "The glory of the Lord has risen upon you. For behold the darkness shall cover the earth and gross darkness, the people."

In the last 10-15 years, darkness has become increasingly prevalent. Unfortunately, America leads the way in much of the perversion and disgusting sin being released to the rest of the world. Canada is becoming a leader as well. We need to pray and ask for God's mercy on those nations. I believe we have a short timeframe and window of mercy for the Church in America to rise up. If the Church doesn't arise, it'll be over for the United States of America.

That's the Church's fault for not being salt and light, not the fault of the world. God says this darkness is coming, but the caveat is that the Lord will rise over you. We have "Your light is come." Revelation has come! The transforming understanding of your identity in Christ is necessary for you to shine like Jesus on the Mount of Transfiguration.

Because you've received that revelation, His glory now rests upon you. God is going to arise over you and under the shadow of His wings you shall trust. The "hem of the tallith" are called the wings. In the bridal covenant when the bride and groom came together, the groom would put the "tallith" over the bride and under the wings of that tallith she could now rest, assured and safe and in trust. Again, we're fusing together!

This is a Season of Grace and Revelation

We're in a season of profound intimacy that's drawing us into a place we've never known. Our hearts, by the grace of God, yearn for this. It's a gift of God when we hunger for God. We can't judge those who are not hungry because God has graced us to be forerunners to step into a place some want but don't know about yet. Seeing the Light come upon you will provoke them to jealousy.

The Light is come. I had these revelations 10 years ago, but at that time the Church wasn't ready for it. 15 years ago, they wanted to lock me up over this! 20 years ago, you didn't dare say anything like this or you'd never be invited into a church again. Remember the video I told you about with Brother Grubbs who carried this revelation back in the '50s? He was ostracized throughout his Christian life yet was effective in ministry because he kept following God. He and his wife were severely wounded because of the rejection, but they forgave and kept pressing on. We're in a season where grace and revelation are being released. Your light has come, so arise and shine!

Scripture goes on to say, "His glory will be seen upon you" (Isaiah 60:2). This is different than praying and seeing miracles happen. People can see God's manifestation of His glory in that way, but I'm referring to His glory being seen upon you. Not around you, but upon you. There's a difference! The Church and the world will see God's glory upon you.

If not this year, then early next year, major news outlets will begin to report on strange happenings in the Church because the presence of God will be there. It's going to become so predominant that they'll have to report it because everybody will be talking about it. This will come with a full spectrum of responses including ridicule, mockery, awe and respect.

Don't worry about what people say; hear what God is saying. There will be attacks on churches, but the people will be untouched because they'll be abiding under the shadow. Thousands will fall on one side and ten thousand on your right side but it won't come near you (Psalm 91:7).

We were invited to a church in Indonesia some years ago at Christmastime. Preparing for their Christmas celebration, they decorated the platform with wrapped packages and boxes for the kids coming to sing and worship God. Unbeknownst to them, two Muslim ladies had snuck in and placed bombs under those packages. They were in the middle of worship and praising God when suddenly, the bombs blew the windows out, destroying the furniture and everything inside the church. The first responders arrived, looked around and asked, "Where are the bodies?"

The explosion and shrapnel from the explosion had gone through the clothing of the people but never touched their skin. They, including the children, were untouched and not even traumatized. That's a powerful example of abiding under the shadow of the Almighty. When they asked if we wanted to minister at their church, I said, "As long as it's not Christmas, I'm there!"

Recognize as you study Scripture that darkness was the original state of everything. The physical description of darkness is the absence of light. The spiritual representation of darkness is life without light or the life of God. You were once darkness but now you're light because you have the life of the presence of the life of God. It's time to shine!

Scientifically, darkness can't be measured, contained, or taken into a laboratory to test in any way. Photons of light, however, can be examined and measured. Darkness is life apart from the light and purpose of God. Life cannot exist without light.

Somebody told me that the deepest depths of the ocean have no light and yet there's still life. They've tested that theory and found photons of light even in that darkness, not to the measure we have above the water of course, but light is present in that darkness. Life cannot exist without light, yet the end result of life without light is eternal separation from light.

Let me share some basic facts about light from physics. Light is electro-magnetic radiation emanating from a source. Light extends in the color spectrum from red to violet. Both electro-magnetic radiation including light and God exist outside of time.

Light is one of the major features of near-death experiences. People who have had near-death experiences report that they're drawn upward toward the light, some to eternity with God, some to judgment. God is light.

The created realm of light is a construct of the physical world, light, time, and space. But the realm of the spirit is superior and far above the construct that we know as the natural. You're not of the created order of light, but of God, the Creator who is light.

God transcends the created order and has authority over the created. He operates from a higher level of physics, so to speak, or laws governing what's possible and not possible in the construct of the natural realm. Therefore, nothing is impossible to one who believes.

Jesus ascended in the clouds, which is of a higher order. The law of gravity says you can't do it, and everybody understands that airplanes require lift to rise. The law of lift doesn't explain how Jesus ascended, yet Jesus overcame gravity, space, and time when He went from this dimension to another.

In the Span of His Hand

Everything that God created fits in the span of His hand.

"Who hath measured the waters in the hollow of his hand, and meted out heaven with the span, and comprehended the dust of the earth in a measure, and weighed the mountains in scales, and the hills in a balance?" (Isaiah 40:12, KJV).

That's the construct: all of space, all of time, all of created light, everything from the minutest molecule to the biggest planet, all fits in the span of His hand. David said, "What is man that you are mindful of him? Or the son of man, that you have given him dominion over all the works of your hand?" (Psalm 8:4).

That should jolt you! Everything He created fits in the span of your hand, and He's given you dominion over all the works of His hand. That truth has been working in me ever since the Lord gave me this revelation. Reshma and I have talked about, thought about, meditated on, and studied this, and I still can't get my grey matter around that truth!

About five years ago, I was caught up into Paradise and found myself before God the Father who was walking through the Garden. I thought, *Wait a minute. You're supposed to be on the throne!*

I heard my inner man say, *No, it's finished! It's finished. God sees the end from the beginning.*

As He walked along, I saw that He was holding something, but I couldn't see what it was. Finally, I saw the construct and everything He had created in the span of His hand, which kept expanding, changing, and morphing. All He held was singing and flashes of light beamed. Looking at this wonder, I felt His joy and His smile.

With His left hand He turned, grabbed my right hand and put all He held in my hand. I could only watch and experience this in complete awe. He said, "Tell My people it is time they understood who they truly are." Then I found myself back in my room. At times I still feel and see what He showed me that day, awed that God the Father would release such a revelation.

"Why?" I asked Him.

"It is coming to the end of the age," He said. "What My people do not understand is the authority I am releasing to them at the end of the age. It is far beyond anything they can ever ask, think, or imagine. But it will only operate under submission to My authority."

Every August, a meteor shower comes through the western hemisphere where we live. Reshma and I love to sit together in lounge chairs to gaze at the stars, count satellites as they pass by, and watch shooting stars. One day we even saw the space shuttle go by! Seeing that majesty reminds me of God, so I can communicate with Him in that place. For me, it's like a prayer closet.

He said, "What My people do not understand is the authority I am releasing to them at the end of the age. But it will only operate under submission to My authority."

As we watched, the Lord dropped one word into my heart: Remember. I said, "Reshma, I think God is challenging me to practice my faith. Let's do it!"

Pointing at the night sky, I said, "Father, we command a shooting star to come out here." We waited and watched for about 30 seconds, when a bright shooting star passed by, leaving us speechless.

Most people would likely believe this was a coincidence, but I had a witness and remember thinking it would be great to have a confirmation or a second witness. In my heart, I said, "Father can I do it one more time?"

Getting an internal nod from Him, I said, "In the Name of Jesus, I command another shooting star." Instantly another star shot across the sky!

We returned inside the house with the fear of the Lord in our hearts. I've never tried speaking to the stars since because we haven't had a release to do so, nor do we play with these things.

The Lord spoke to me and said, "That was easy! That's the easy stuff. Wait till you see what's coming!"

Somebody said, "The Bible tells us to raise the dead, but what if they've been cremated?"

I said, "That's not too hard for God!" You're going see that! What about somebody that's been blown up? That's not too hard for God either! He keeps track of every atom and molecule in your body. We're going to see and walk in what defies science and comprehension.

Understanding Light

Light exhibits in uncanny, unexplainable awareness or consciousness of its surroundings. Scientists have split-light experiments where they split a photon of light by sending it through two different holes in an object (much like if you had rays of light coming through two different holes in a piece of paper). The split light goes in different directions yet, on the other side of the split, it comes back together. They can't explain it and don't understand it except to say that light is consciously aware of itself. This is created light.

The human spirit has a God-size hole, which is a picture of the split-light. Your spirit is trying to draw you back to the Source of all light. This awareness on light's part occurs instantaneously, faster than the speed of light as light and God are outside of time. In creation, when the Lord spoke, "Let there be!" an explosion took place as 186,300 miles per second was released from Him.

According to Einstein's theory of relativity and light, if you take a spaceship and send it at almost a quarter of the speed of light, or half the speed of light, it could return 50 or 100 years later and you wouldn't have aged seven years. But if you reach the speed of light, time stops and you stop aging. You travel so fast when you reach the speed of light that you go beyond the speed of light and into the realm of ETERNITY, which is the realm of God.

When you visit heaven, you're moving faster than the speed of light. When you step from one geographic point on the earth to another, that's an application of light. You become walking science labs! This is important because if you get a simple glimpse of light and understand who you are in Christ, it demystifies this and gives you more understanding so you can have a greater confidence in what God is trying to release.

The Lord releases light, revelation, understanding, insight, and intimacy to us because each facet of the revelation of light conforms us to that light. In this hour, when He says, "Your light has come," there's going be an explosion of this reality. It's not necessary to understand all of this, but since I'm called to teach about this revelation, I'm giving you more than you really need to know. These become tools that will help you grow and focus your heart more intentionally on what God is trying to communicate in this hour.

You are light—not natural light or created light. We're created in His image so our spirit man is creator-light, if you will. That's why He's giving you the creator ability: What you speak, you can become.

Scripture says that God upholds all things by the Word of His power (Hebrews 1:3). Dr. David Van Koevering, a quantum physicist, wrote the Foreword in my book *Gazing into Glory*. Dr. Van Koevering told me there's nothing solid in creation. We all flash in and out of existence, and if God removed the upholding power of His Word, we would all vanish.

As Dr. Van Koevering and I talked about this and he described something to me, I said, "Oh! that's in the Bible."

"Really?" he said. "Where?"

This is how God marries the Word in physics. Dr. Van Koevering was reading the Old Covenant one day and read about Joshua picking up a stone and saying, "Let this stone be a witness, it has heard all the words the Lord has said to us" (see Joshua 24:27).

What? He thought.

"Wait a minute, matter has memory!" he said. "That's why you have hard drives. Matter has memory." He started digging into the physics behind this revelation.

Before he died, Dr. Van Koevering had over 600 patents in physics. He invented the touch screen on your phones and iPad, but other companies had more financial backing than he had to fight for it, so his ideas were stolen from him. He invented the electronic keyboard, starting with the Korg Synthesizer back in the '70s. He had a brilliant mind! Even more amazing is that he never studied physics; he was simply a genius who loved physics. He could also play any musical instrument known to man. His house was like a museum of bizarre instruments, all of which he could play.

Dr. Van Koevering began to work on and meditate on the physics of matter and discovered how to extract the memory out of matter. He said the technology didn't exist until years later but is now in place. His plan was to go to Israel and build the machine that could extract memory from matter. When he talked with lawyers, judges and friends, one judge said to him, "Do you know what that's going to do to the legal realm? If there's a crime committed, we'll only have to say, 'Give me your necklace. Let's see what actually happened,' and it will all have been recorded with video and audio."

Memory of everything that was ever said or done in a room is recorded in the walls. What would happen if you examined the Via Dolorosa? Dr. Van Koevering said he's done this research and utilized it on certain things, yet one thing confounds the science: When he applied the blood of Jesus over anything, it had no memory. Wow! Apply the blood of Jesus! That's powerful and understandable as an application of light, frequency, resonance, and color.

Reflectors

Light travels from its source and immediately reflects off every object with which it comes in contact. You're called to reflect the glory of God, which will be seen on you at the end of the age as we're getting close to God. Consider Moses when he descended from Mount Sinai after being in God's presence. The people said, "Cover your face! We can't look!"

Moses had spent so much time in the presence of God—who is light and glory—that he began to reflect that glory. The level of intimacy available to the children of God at the end of the age will cause you to glow. No other generation has been given this. That's why Jesus began to glow from the inside out while in communion with the Father on the Mount of Transfiguration.

The level of relationship and intimacy we're going to share with the Father, Jesus, and the Holy Spirit in this hour is the natural byproduct of that intimacy. We're going to glow with the glory! It will be seen upon you, and you'll be known as the people of the Light.

A colorless object will register as black in our brains. A white object reflects all colors of the rainbow at the same time into our eyes. We think of the objects as having color when, in fact, they're simply reflecting that particular wavelength of light into our eyes.

This is like the seven spirits of God: The interaction and manifestation of the Spirit of the Lord and the Spirits of Wisdom, Understanding, Counsel, Might, Knowledge, and Fear of the Lord. When the Lord is working with you and you need wisdom, say: "Lord, I need the Spirit of Wisdom or the Spirit of Might." Suddenly, you'll be able to connect with that wavelength, facet, and frequency of God and begin to walk in it.

Do you remember the example of the FM radio dial I mentioned earlier? It can be likened to God tuning you. Tune your spirit into the proper God frequency and then walk in it. Exercising your faith or taking steps of faith will help tune your spirit into the frequency of the realm or dimension of the spirit so you can walk in it. This already belongs to you, but you must learn to discipline yourself to tune into the wavelength or frequency.

Cameras can catch supernatural things because they pick up a greater spectrum of frequency of light than the natural eye picks up. The spirit realm is a different frequency of existence around us right now. As you learn to walk with God, your eyes attune to that realm and frequency. Your senses can also be attuned, according to Scripture: "Taste and see that the Lord is good" (Psalm 34:8).

Identify with who you are, not what you hope to become. The only "becoming" needed is you becoming aware and releasing yourself to the processes of God. You already are what God says you are.

Light is only the visible spectrum of electromagnetic radiation. Other forms of radiation from weakest to strongest are radio waves, microwave, infrared, visible or white light, ultraviolet, x-rays, and gamma rays. This world is inundated with radiation, especially in the electronic age. You can't get away from radio frequencies, as they're passing through us always.

Visible light is normally emitted from a source of heat like the sun using fission, to create a tremendous amount of heat giving off light. This is a picture of God, a consuming fire—Light. Heat and light are almost always simultaneous. At times in my early walk with the Lord, I'd get so hot, I'd drip with sweat when the presence of God came over me, and I didn't understand it.

As stated earlier, light travels at 186,300 miles per second, and God created us in the same way He created light, which travels in particle form. Most noteworthy about this type of travel is that it's helical in nature. DNA is a helix, and light looks exactly the same. That's not because light is like you, it means you are like light. You're created in God's image.

**Identify with who you are, not what you hope to become.
You already are what God says you are.**

He created the very fabric of our being and existence in tandem with His light. The entrance of His Word gives light because we work in tandem. When you speak the Word of God under the unction of the Holy Spirit of God into your body, the helix of light and helix of the natural body come into alignment with God who is the helix of light.

God's Word is a force that's released to impact, tear down, build up, and create. Because He is light—the helix of light interacts with the created realm and does something to it. That's why we're in the season when we're going to see even those who have been cremated brought back to life. When the body is cremated, it changes form, yet is still molecules and particles. It's nothing for God to convert it back to its original form.

You've heard of people receiving teeth in meetings where the presence of God is manifest. The tooth may be gone, but the memory of the tooth (remember, matter has memory) is still there, so God recreates it. The memory of a missing arm is still there, so God can recreate it. That's what happens with creative miracles. The memory is in the DNA of the individual, and the original Architect knows how to make it work.

When the Lord began to teach me about translation by faith, He gave me some understanding about this. Remember the example of my friend and I traveling by car and laying our hands on the dashboard to pray? Though a six-hour drive of over 350 miles in the natural, we arrived in less than 90 minutes even though we had stopped for an hour, had dinner, and filled the car with gas.

When I asked God what had happened, He said, "You learned that the shortest distance between two points is a straight line." Then He added, "Unless you are God."

He shortened the straight line and said the shortest distance between two points is already being there! That's when I started to study physics because I was expecting a lesson in translation. I got a lesson, but it wasn't a lesson I had expected! Until God directed me to study light, this didn't make sense. Yet now, it makes perfect sense. The faster you get to the speed of the light, the shorter the distance is between two points.

People have said there are only certain geographic regions where translation can take place. Yes, there are geographic places like this throughout Scripture like the Mount of Transfiguration and Mount Sinai. That's why the Lord said to tear down the high places because they were thin places that enabled people to cross from one realm to the other. Study it in Hebrews!

If you know your identity in Christ, He doesn't have to go to a geographic carrier to be manifested. You're in Him, so you don't have to either.

The astrophysicist John Gribbin summarized it like this: An electromagnetic wave is everywhere along its path, everywhere in the universe, it's omnipresent at once. Or you can say that distance doesn't exist for an electromagnetic wave, which is light. Or in another way, everything in the universe, past, present, and future is connected to everything else, by a web of electromagnetic radiation that sees everything at once.

Scripture says God knows the end from the beginning and holds all things, including space and time, in the span of His hand.

He knows what He's called you to do and can see the goal, destiny or scroll of your life all at once. He speaks over you what He sees. But you have to make a choice to cooperate with Him.

Antwerp in the Middle Ages

While in prayer and worship in my study a couple of years ago, I suddenly found myself standing in the street in a downpour. The surroundings were filthy and the streets muddy. Looking ahead, I saw two oxen pulling a big wagon down the street. A little boy sat not far away in the mud crying. I thought, Where am I? What's happened?

Instantly, I knew I was in Antwerp, Belgium during the Middle Ages. Walking along, getting soaked with mud covering my shoes, I came to grips with what was happening. Moved with compassion I went over to the little boy and asked, "Why are you crying? What's the matter?"

"My mommy is dying, and I can't see her," he said. "They won't let me in the house."

"Take me to her," I told him.

He looked at me fearfully but with hope, as he wanted to see his mother before she died. Grabbing my hand, he pulled me down a back street and we walked on cobbled stones that led to the door of a simple, humble home.

As the boy opened the door, I saw a bed in the middle of the floor and a man sitting next to the bed. The man shouted, "No, don't come in! It's the plague!"

"It's okay," I told him. We came into the house but the boy stood next to the door, afraid his dad would send him out again.

I saw somebody standing in the corner and later understood it was an angel. The father was uncomfortable when I came in and stood at the foot of the bed so I said, "The Lord sent me."

As I shared the Gospel of Jesus with them, I could discern that the mother was aware but weak. I asked, "Ma'am, would you like to accept Jesus?"

Nodding, she said, "Yes."

The man and his young son wept. The angel standing in the corner smiled and looked on.

"Let's hold hands," I said to the family. We joined hands as I led them in a prayer of salvation. Then I said, "Now, in the Name of Jesus, I command life back into your body."

The woman sat up, instantly healed!

Suddenly, I was back home again. "What was that, Lord? I asked. "That was really strange and outside of anything I've ever heard of." Then I said, "Lord, was that true?"

"Google it," He said.

When I googled Antwerp in the Middle Ages, plague, I learned that the bubonic plague started in the Jewish quarter. They blamed the Jews and kicked them out of Antwerp.

Shocked, I said, "But Lord, what was that You just showed me?"

I needed to discuss this encounter with someone, so I called Neville Johnson. "You know," Neville explained, "that's happened to me too, but I don't share it because people can't handle it."

"Yes," I said, "but you're old and wise, and I'm young and stupid."

Scripture says that John was on the Island of Patmos and in the spirit on the Lord's day when the Lord took him forward in time to show him the future. Moses said, "Lord, show me Your glory." He saw the hind parts of God because he couldn't look onto the face of God at that time. This was an application of the glory where he saw from the creation up to that very moment.

Trying to process and understand this, I told the Lord, "But Lord, they're already dead."

"From My perspective," He said, "before the foundation of the world, it was already known that a man from 2015 would be sent back to the Middle Ages to interact with a woman on her deathbed and that she would be saved." That knocked me over. Study light!

Be warned however: I didn't initiate this encounter and don't suggest you try to do so either. God is sovereign, and if He chooses to do something, follow Him and obey Him.

John was in the spirit when God initiated an encounter with him. You can't just decide, "Well, I'm going to go to hell and save my family." No, you're not. That's plain stupid and unbiblical. You Must be led of the Spirit according to the Scriptures. your emotions, not your desires, not your wants, but by the Spirit of God. Anything beyond that is foolishness and will get you into real trouble.

Again: The Lord God is Light. He is not created light but is light and the Creator of light. He is everywhere at once; His light travels faster than the speed of light. He's already where He needs to be at any place and any time. He's the Alpha and the Omega. In translation by faith, this understanding of light will give you a powerful foundation from which to move forward.

Genesis 1:1-2 says,

> "In the beginning God created the heaven and the earth. And the earth was without form, and void; and darkness was upon the face of the deep. And the Spirit of God moved upon the face of the waters" (KJV).

God's answer to darkness was light! "And God said, 'Let there be light' and there was light. And God saw the light, that it was good: and God divided the light from the darkness" (Genesis 1:3-4, KJV).

The answer to all darkness in your life is light. God is light, so the answer to anything in your life is God. Yet, we have a tendency, because we dwell in the natural realm, to look for a solution in the natural realm.

SUPERNATURAL SUPPLY

We have a friend who is a well-known, successful real estate agent. Because he was the go-to person for selling multi-million-dollar properties, he became very wealthy. One day, the Lord said to him: "I want you to leave the business and trust Me for your income."

The husband and wife prayed together and obeyed God's direction. After a short period of time, their money and investments were gone, and they sat looking at the mountain of bills coming due.

His wife said, "Well, Lord, I'm doing what You said to do." She developed a bill-paying system where, if a bill was due on a Monday, she put it in the Monday slot, and for bills due on Tuesday, she'd put the bill in the Tuesday slot, and so on.

Each day she prayed, and the day before a bill was due, she'd say, "Lord, this bill is due tomorrow." When she opened the envelope

The answer to all darkness in your life is light. God is light, so the answer to anything in your life is God.

the next morning, the money to pay the bill was in the slot. This continued for months as God paid their bills. You can't do something like this unless God tells you to do it, but He was teaching her a lesson: "I am your source. I am the answer to your need even when it comes to provision."

Reshma and I have learned to give, and we know God's going to give us back 100-fold blessing as there's truth in the Word. But, be led of the Spirit and not by a formula. Don't manipulate God! Learn to give because you love God, not because you want something back. If you're walking in accordance with what God tells you, Scripture says that God's blessings will overtake you! God can and will provide.

During a revival in Indonesia, the people had no food so they gathered the family, put the pots on the table and prayed. When they opened the lid, God had supernaturally filled the pot with food, always enough for each meal, never more and never less. We have a God who knows how to take care of His children, and we must learn to lean upon that truth.

"And God said, 'Let there be light': and there was light" (Genesis 1:3, KJV).

We fly frequently and have racked up many air miles. I'm tired of flying the airlines because they're always coming over the intercom to say, "Please put your seat belts on. We're about to hit a rough patch."

As we fly, I've learned over the years to say to the wind, "Peace, be still," and immediately the turbulence stops. While I was learning, studying, and meditating on light one day during a flight, the aircraft started bouncing around in strong turbulence. When I said, "I release the light," it was as if an instant beam of light went out from me and in front of the aircraft, making the air pressure become smooth as glass. Light is the answer.

When my Dad and I used to pastor churches, he'd call somebody who needed prayer up to the front. As he talked with them, he'd say to the congregation, "Everybody, stretch out your hands," then he'd keep talking for another 10 minutes.

As this continued, I'd get in the flesh. Frustrated, I'd think, *Why do you do this? You're the one praying for her, you should just pray because this is ridiculous.* But then I'd have to say, "God, forgive me. I repent. I'm under authority, but please straighten him out."

One day my Dad said, "Everybody stretch out your hand." I stood in awe as I saw that everybody's hands were radiating light. "Wow!" I said. "Light sabers!"

I suddenly understood that we were corporately releasing light into the darkness that needed to be addressed. My dad had taken it even further, saying that when you go into a place that's darkness, without saying a word, you can simply stand there and release the light. As you release that glory, something powerful happens!

Light accomplishes three things in the natural: It provides energy, it reveals through reflection, and it is the most accurate measuring device. A laser measuring device measures precisely. Much like when you stand next to God, the most accurate measuring device, your frailties and weaknesses are revealed. But in God it's redemptive because you can repent and step into that wholeness He offers you.

You can say: "I don't know how to walk in the spirit and I don't know how to translate, but I trust You, Lord." Or, "I don't know how to pray and I don't know what to do, but I trust You, Lord." Regardless of what you do in this world, you have an audience of One. According to the Word of God and the God of the Word, you already measure up to Him. You're created in His image and you are light. The devil wants you to think you're no good, or you can't, or it's too hard, or you're not educated enough. All you need is faith in God!

Ignorant and unlearned men in the first century church turned the world upside down. God used fishermen, tax collectors, publicans, sinners, not well educated, filthy rich, or good looking. Dependence upon God positions you for the power, presence, and person of God.

Light Exposes

Light illuminates every hidden obstacle in your path. In 1978 I was going to Bible College while working at TBN. My best friend from high school and I hadn't seen each other for about a year, so I said, "I have a long weekend coming up, so come on down!"

He flew in on a Thursday, and on Friday I explained to him that my shift started at 3 o'clock, but I'd get off at midnight and be home by 1 am. I said, "Make yourself at home, and then we can have the long weekend together."

I went to work, then came home to my small one-bedroom apartment. He was sleeping on the couch because I wasn't going to give up my bed. Coming into my apartment, I thought, I'll be quiet and keep the lights off so I don't wake him up. Even with the lights off I thought I knew the path through my own apartment. But suddenly and unexpectedly I tripped over the coffee table. Bam!

He might have moved the coffee table for some reason, I thought. I went another way and tripped over the chair! Every way I moved, I hit something. Being in pain from smashing into the furniture made me angry. I turned on the lights to discover that he had rearranged everything in my apartment. I was afraid to look in the kitchen cupboards! I said, "What are you doing?"

"You told me to make myself at home," he said. "I don't like how you decorated it. Don't you think this looks much better?"

I said, "Just don't touch anything!" This is a good example of how light comes to expose darkness and obstacles.

Matthew 5:14 says, "Ye are the light of the world. A city that is set on a hill cannot be hid" (KJV). A city set on a mountain cannot be hidden. True light can never be hidden. Evident to all, pure light has no darkness in it. Natural light can have a shadow or degrees of illumination, but pure light has none. This may be difficult to imagine until you've seen it, but there are no shadows in heaven because everything is permeating or releasing the light.

This is a picture of how we're to walk in this life: No shadows, no shades of purity or mixture. James 1:17 says, "Every good gift and every perfect gift is from above, and cometh down from the Father of lights, with whom is no variableness, neither shadow of turning" (KJV).

Shadows cause you to turn and stumble. God says you are light and that light cannot be hidden. If that light cannot be hidden, why don't more people recognize us as Christians in everyday life? It's because we want to fit in and don't want to be that light.

God's light has come, His glory is going to rise upon you, and you're going to understand when people begin to come. You may wonder why many will come to you. They'll come because they want the light!

As you bask in the atmosphere of the Holy Spirit, you'll receive something because more is caught than taught. When you're anointed with oil, they smear on the oil. When you're in the atmosphere of the Holy Spirit, you're smeared with the Holy Spirit and the release of revelation. I encourage you to linger in an atmosphere where the anointing begins to shift and change you.

When I was growing up, my dad was a leader in the Full Gospel Businessmen's Association. When they hosted these great banquets and conferences, they'd always tell me to go to the youth meeting. I didn't want to go to the youth meeting! Back then, youth meetings were like, "Kumbaya, my Lord"—boring!

I wanted to attend the real meeting where these old guys were sharing testimonies of raising the dead! When they'd go out after the meeting to visit and have coffee and a piece of pie, I always went. I'd quietly sit in the corner, not interrupting or saying anything, but soaking it all in. I couldn't get enough!

I remember a forerunner named Jim Spillman. He'd be at the podium speaking, "And the Lord sayeth," and the whole room would collapse because of the anointing. Over they'd go, just like dominoes!

I'd say, "Wow! I want that, God!"

"You already have it," He replied.

"How does it work?" I'd ask. He would never tell me because I wasn't ready yet. I'd watch these men and women of God over time as I sat in the corner listening and learning.

Over the course of my life, as God has released revelation about translation by faith to me, He'd take me back to that place and say, "Remember: This is where it was imparted to you." They didn't pray for me but I caught more than I was taught. Whenever you get an opportunity to be around men and women of God, grab hold of it. They don't bring that presence; God's presence comes and permeates the atmosphere. He is living proof.

Moses' Shining Face

"It came about when Moses was coming down from Mount Sinai (and the two tablets of the testimony were in

Moses' hand as he was coming down from the mountain), that Moses did not know that the skin of his face shone because of his speaking with Him" (Exodus 34:29, NASB).

Moses came down from Mt. Sinai with the two tablets of the testimony in his hands. As he descended the mountain, Moses didn't know that the skin of his face began to shine while he talked with God. When Aaron and the children of Israel saw Moses and saw his face shining, they were afraid to come near him. When Moses called them, Aaron and the rulers of the congregation returned and talked with him, but said, "Cover your face." He had spent so much time in the manifest presence of God, they were unable to look on him.

What took place then is beginning to take place now, being activated at the end of the age. We're going to spend so much time in the manifest presence of God, we're going to shine. Moses was under a lesser covenant with lesser release of revelation and insight.

We have a better covenant! Under our covenant, God has written everything on the tablets of our hearts. How much more should we be glowing! The Lord dwells within us. He's not on the outside trying to get in. He's on the inside trying to get out!

Those in the occult and witchcraft arena see the light in us. A witch doctor in Northern Alaska was a shaman, and for a fee you could pay him to curse and wreak havoc in a person's life. A missionary who attended Full Gospel Businessmen's meetings came to the area and was winning people to the Lord. When a particular man's wife accepted Jesus, the husband became terribly upset, so he went to this shaman and said, "Here's the fee. I want you to either kill that missionary or chase him out of here."

The shaman agreed, then performed a ritual where he spiritually left his body and went to the house where the missionary was staying. He tried to look in but couldn't move beyond the radiance of the glory of God because of the light emanating from the missionary. Unable to get in, he returned home.

The next day he walked four miles to the missionary's house and said, "What is the power you have? It's stronger than anything I've ever seen."

The missionary led the shaman to Jesus, the source of that power. You must know your identity in Christ! No weapon formed against you will prosper unless you allow it.

In Exodus 3:1, Moses was tending the flock of his father-in-law, Jethro, the priest of the Median. "Now Moses was pasturing the flock of Jethro, his father-in-law, the priest of Midian; and he led the flock to the west side of the wilderness and came to Horeb, the mountain of God" (NASB).

Tending sheep is a picture and metaphor of "pastoral care." Notice the sheep didn't belong to Moses, but he protected them, saw that they were fed and watered, and stewarded over them. The sheep in your churches don't belong to you. They belong to the Father. Your stewardship is to see that they flourish.

In Christendom, some think they're building their own kingdom or group. We say, "Don't go listen to that person or don't go over here or over there." Yet we'll steal anybody to make our flock grow. No!

My dad had wisdom about pastoral stewardship. He'd say, "They're not my sheep. If they come or if they go, it doesn't matter because they belong to God." Pay attention to this!

Moses led the flock to the back of the desert and came to Horeb, the mountain of God. The angel of the Lord appeared to him in a flame of fire from the midst of the bush and he looked, and behold, the bush was not consumed. Moses said, "I will now turn aside and see this great sight, why the bush does not burn."

At times in your life, you've been going in one direction, but then comes a moment of turning aside. What you've always known to do in ministry and in your walk with God is changing direction, and now, it's time to turn aside. God wants to release a new thing to you!

When the Lord saw that Moses turned aside to look, God called to him from the midst of the bush and said, "Moses! Moses!"

There's an interesting insight into this from the Hebrew mindset. God called Moses' name twice, and two is the number of "witness." This says: Pay attention, Moses! This is significant!

Moses responded, "Here I am."

God said, "Don't come near here. Take your sandals off your feet for the place where you stand is holy ground." You know the story. Though Moses was called from birth, God commissioned him at 80 years of age. Take note: Being called to something doesn't mean you're there already. The call and commissioning are always seasons apart. Notice that Elijah didn't come on the scene until 1 Kings 17 when he was a 30-year-old man.

As you turn aside to this new thing God wants to release, you'll notice that from the moment of encounter to the moment of activation to where you begin to walk this out is as quick as the snap of your fingers. The Lord spoke to Moses and said, "This is how it's going to be done. Now do it!" And so, he began that journey.

Clothed with Light

Psalm 104:1-2 says,

"Bless the Lord, O my soul. O Lord my God, thou art very

great; thou art clothed with honour and majesty. Who coverest thyself with light as with a garment: who stretchest out the heavens like a curtain" (KJV).

God is clothed with light as a garment. In Genesis 1 God declares the end from the beginning. God created Adam in His image and likeness and was clothed with light.

In the Garden of Eden, Adam and Eve were clothed with light, as with a garment. They didn't know nakedness because they were clothed with light. When they divorced themselves from the covering of God and chose to eat the forbidden fruit, the garment of light was removed. Their spirit that had been in the pre-eminent position, suddenly atrophied, and then they were naked. Through the second Adam (Jesus), God re-breathed life into your spirit, returning it to the pre-eminent position. In the spirit you're already clothed with light as with a garment. This has everything to do with translation because light is everywhere.

Steps of faith to practice engaging the realm of the spirit and translation by faith offers a grace season now to practice and become proficient. The time will come to enter into the fullness, and you'll say, "Lord, what are we doing today?" instead of, "Lord, do You want to come along?" You're under authority—HIS authority—so grab hold of the grace God is extending to practice and become proficient.

We received a report from a young lady in Germany who heard this teaching last year and was believing God for activation in her life. She and her friend were talking about translation and the scriptures that had been shared in the school as they were walking to the train station. They had planned to take the train from their town to a town located three or four stations away, a 45-minute train ride.

As this young lady told her friend how translation works, they walked into the train station to buy their ticket. When they walked through the door to get onto the train, they actually stepped out at their destination! Shocked, her friend said, "Does this happen often to you?"

"More than it has happened before!" she responded. She testified to translating as she drove her car, starting out, and then arriving at her destination in moments!

Another young newly saved woman in Germany had been reading my book *Prophetic Promise of the 7th Day* that she had received from the woman who led her to the Lord. Within a week of reading the book, she was translating all over the place because she had no excess baggage of religion. She simply believed, received, and said, "Okay!"

There's a grace upon the Church right now. If you'll say, "Father, I don't understand, but I receive it. I don't understand it all, but I receive it," He'll respond!

My wife Reshma's favorite testimony is about walking in translation by faith. Here's her story:

I love to share this most amazing story as it demonstrates God's mercy, grace, and love. It also encourages us in what we've been doing with the Translation School. Sometimes, while serving the Lord, going here and there and doing what God has called us to do, we grow weary. Some people might ask, "Is it really making a difference?" Some places we go, people receive us, while other places, people think we're crazy and treat us differently.

As Christians, especially in full time ministry, the enemy attacks on many fronts and often uses people in those attacks. After an experience that left us troubled in our hearts, we were out of state for ministry, when we received an email from a pastor located about 21 miles north of us. "Brother Bruce," he wrote, "you don't know me, but I know you, and I know your dad. I've seen you minister and I want to share something with you. Something supernatural is happening in our church."

He went on to say, "There's a couple in our church who just love the Lord. The wife went to an auction because the church had donated all our materials, auctioning anything at all to generate some money..." He explained that one lady got Bruce's book *Gazing into Glory* at the auction, brought it home and gave it to her husband, thinking that he'd like it.

One day they were lying in bed, reading. She was reading another book and her husband was reading Bruce's *Gazing into Glory*. When he came to a place where translation and the supernatural are mentioned, he prayed, "God, I don't know if this is true, but if it's true, I want it."

As he later testified to us, suddenly two angels came into the room, picked him up, and took him up to the ceiling while he looked down and could see his body still in the bed reading the book.

The angels then took him out through the roof and into the air where he was looking down at someone's house at nighttime. When he saw the house, he knew everything about the house and the people in it, including their names, who they were, their beliefs, and the problems they faced. He even knew their dog's name! In an instant he received supernatural knowledge about this family.

Then the Spirit of the Lord took him over the city where he had supernatural knowledge of every person in every house and car. Then the angels took him over the county, and again he received instant knowledge about every person in every house and car. When the angels took him over the state of Washington, he encountered the same supernatural knowledge of each one.

He asked the Lord, "Lord, why are You showing me this?"

The Lord said, "You wanted to know if My Word is true."

This encounter dramatically changed his life. When he gave the book to his friend, without telling him about his personal experience, his friend experienced the exact supernatural encounter!

His testimony about his supernatural encounter encouraged us, and God sent it to us after we had faced discouragement. We said, "Thank you! And thank You, Lord, for encouraging us!" May that encourage you too!

Though part of the Christian experience is facing attacks of the enemy that often come through people, we're thankful that God always sends us testimonies like this to encourage us. When we saw this man again, he was still so excited that he told us his story again. A pastor today, he and his wife have a wonderful fellowship. The Lord is doing amazing things in their midst with signs, wonders and miracles. -Reshma

God is releasing revelation, and this testimony demonstrates how simple the process is: Saying honestly to the Lord, "I don't know if this is real, but if it is, I want it!" This man didn't only lend the book to his friend, he said that every person he gave the book *Gazing into Glory*, began to experience supernatural encounters. So, I asked him, "Can I have that book back?"

Walking in the Supernatural is Available to All!

Because of the power of the testimony, we're compiling a book of testimonies from the Schools of the Supernatural that will be an addendum to what we've already documented. Because the testimony of Jesus is the Spirit of the Prophecy, testimonies are prophesies that will be released into other lives to bring encouragement.

Chapter Ten

YOU ARE LIGHT

You've been called to be light to this dark world while it's day, and Jesus said, walk while you have the light (see John 9:4). This word "walk" literally means to tread around proudly. Not with pride or arrogance, but with an assurance of who you are in Christ. You don't have to be the church mouse, being meek, weak, and scared of your shadow. As I shared earlier, meekness is power under control. You can walk with full confidence in who God says you are.

Some days you may not feel that confident assurance. You may not always feel like you're light, your countenance may not look like you're light, but the Word of God says you are light. Take the report of the Lord and hold on to that, not your circumstances or your feelings. God's Word is Truth!

We don't need to fear the enemy or his tactics, as Jesus called us to be light. When I first started seeing in the realm of the spirit, I saw demons, large and small. Not once did I sense fear in my heart. I'd simply look at them and think, *Oooh, that's really ugly!* or *What is that, Lord?* I didn't say, "There's a demon. Let me get 'em." I'd say,

"Lord, what are You saying?" God has given us the authority in Christ over the demonic, and we have His protection.

Even when they'd run up to me and roar in my face, I'd just go ultra-bright and say, "Use something. Do something. That breath is ugly." I never faced fear, which is by God's grace. Because of the light, demons couldn't get close.

Before I studied light, I used to joke while teaching and say: "I'm going to win a Nobel Prize in physics because I made an astounding discovery. I found something faster than the speed of light in the natural realm. It's Darkness. When you turn on the light, darkness is gone. And if light travels at 186,300 miles a second, darkness goes a bit faster because it's out of here." When you walk into a room, even if it's filled with demons, they press back because of the light of the glory of God. I've seen it. You are light and can walk with full confidence, assurance, and fearless.

Light has and will continue to change your life. We all joke sometimes, saying, "He's not the brightest bulb in the package" but the reality is that you're a bajillion watts because you're created in God's image. When I worked in a television studio, we'd put wire scrims on the studio lights to soften and bring them down to a certain spectrum.

We allow our flesh to be like those scrims, which dull, soften or deaden the light so it's not as effective as it could be. When you learn to release, you remove all hindrances so your light shines. The devil and the spirit realm see your light clearly. You may have heard new age people say, "Oh! You have an aura." The truth is, you do have an aura in the realm of the spirit as light has frequency.

Remember the seven colors? White light is not really white light as it has all colors of the rainbow. It depends on what frequency you're picking up. Neville Johnson said when you walk in self-pity, it emits a frequency, a stench, and color that the devil is attracted to, like flies are attracted to a kill. Self-pity is repugnant to angels in the realm of the spirit so they flee from it. Even if you're a Christian, they'll stand back because they can't stand that stench. Demons, however, love it.

So, how do you get out from under that oppression? Take pills? Of course not! That only exacerbates it and makes it worse. Then you not only have a problem, you have *pharmakeia* and witchcraft to go with it. I'm not saying that medication hasn't helped people, I'm saying there's a better way: His name is Jesus.

You fight, not an external battle but by the blood of Jesus, the Word of God, and by declaring: "I am who God says I am!"

> "Therefore, if anyone is in Christ, he is a new creation; old things have passed away; behold, all things have become new" (2 Corinthians 5:17).

This newness of life is translated, "re-energized," in the Greek and is synonymous with the idea of electrons and light creation. In this newness, all things become new, energized or re-energized. This is the one place you'll find a difference in you between light and light. If the light in you is darkness, how great is that darkness? But when the Spirit of God comes in and re-energizes that light, you're born again in His likeness. Throughout Scripture you are light.

Don't be surprised if you wake up in the middle of the night because it's so bright in your room. When I've said this in the schools, some students have shared that when this happened to them in the middle of the night, they realized the brightness was the light coming from within them!

God always confirms His Word. The Lord energizes our light by allowing His light to enter in. Once we've accepted His light, old things pass away.

Psalm 27:1 describes light, a key factor in earthly survival. It says, "The Lord is my light and my salvation; Whom shall I fear? The Lord is the strength of my life; Of whom shall I be afraid?" Notice that the Lord is my light and because of that light I have salvation. Therefore, I don't have to fear anybody because I'm light, and that light is in me.

A brother I know was witnessing on the streets when some guys robbed him. In this season, the Lord had been teaching him about the angels that accompany him. So, as he was being robbed, he laughed about it, which confused the thugs. When they asked him what was so funny, he said, "Well, you might be able to beat me up, but you can't beat them!" The guys fell silent because his angels suddenly appeared as beings of light. The robbers turned and fled.

Angels are always with you. You can't outrun them as you can't run that fast. Even driving down the road, you can't lose them. No matter how fast you go, they'll still be standing outside the car moving with you. I've thought, *That's not fair. You should at least look like you're running*! You can't translate without angels, as they're right there too. Thank God!

Some years ago, the Lord assigned an angel of revelation to me, and our friends who saw the angel bore witness to it. He's been with me for over 11 years and the things he comes up with are amazing. You can say, "Wow!" but that's not what I say. I'll give away the secret: I've learned to depend upon the Spirit of God. Now, we can choose to walk in the light.

"Your word is a lamp to my feet and a light to my path" (Psalm 119:105).

Everywhere you walk, you walk on the Word. If you're following the Word of God, you're walking the path of light. If you step off the path of light of His Word, you're walking in darkness.

Years ago, we heard teachings on Matthew 7:13 which says, "Broad is the way that leads to destruction, and there are many who go in by it." I had always wondered about that Scripture. It sounds nice, but I wanted to know what it looked like. One day, as I was praying about it, I suddenly saw a tiny thin fiber-optic line going up and into heaven. I'm not a tightrope walker but this was like a strand of hair. God said, "That's the way of life."

Seeing a huge abyss, I said, "Lord, how does anybody get across this?"

He offered no answer. Finally, in desperation, I dropped to my knees and began to pray. Seeing the abyss expand, I knew that the only way across was through humility on my knees and face. We have a choice to make: Will we choose to walk in the light?

John 1:1 says, "In the beginning was the Word, and the Word was with God, and the Word was God." God is light so when God spoke, he released light. When you speak the word, you release light.

> "He was in the beginning with God. All things were made through Him, and without Him nothing was made that has been made. In Him was life, and the life was the light of men. And the light shines in the darkness, and the darkness did not comprehend it. There was a man sent from God, whose name was John. This man came as a witness, to bear witness of the Light, that all through him might

believe. He was not that Light, but was sent to bear witness of that Light" (John 1:2-8).

John was not that Light but was sent to bear witness of that Light. So, at the end of the age, a generation will come in the spirit and power of Elijah just as John did. We're here to bear witness to the light. We have countless messages and sermons about Christ, the cross, the blood and salvation. But how many people go back to the basics: In the beginning, was LIGHT.

Light was rejected.

"That was the true Light which gives light to every man coming into the world. He was in the world, and the world was made through Him, and the world did not know Him. He came to His own, and His own did not receive Him" (John 1:9-11).

You can reject light or receive light.

"But as many as received Him, to them He gave the right to become children of God, to those who believe in His name: who were born, not of blood, nor of the will of the flesh, nor of the will of man, but of God" (John 1:12-13).

God gives us free will to choose Him.

Light became incarnate in Christ.

"And the Word became flesh and dwelt among us, and we beheld His glory, the glory as of the only begotten of the Father, full of grace and truth" (John 1:14).

Some may ask, "Well, if I go in the spirit, is it tangible?" If light can become flesh, you're going to be changed in a moment, in the twinkling of an eye, back to light, yet have a tangible, physical body. When I translated by the spirit to Latvia to minister to the little girl, I knelt down with her, and she leaned up against me and could feel me. I could touch her and talk to her. I opened the door. A spirit can do that because it takes on a different form that has an application and frequency of light that makes it tangible. God's light can be anything, at anytime, anywhere. That's why you don't have to worry about clothes!

Isaiah 60:8 says, "Who are these who fly like a cloud, And like doves to their roosts?" I did word studies on this Scripture, as did my friend Regner Capener, whom I met with to discuss. In Isaiah 60:1-7, instead of "Arise and shine" the original Hebrew says, "Stand up! Accomplish, confirm and decree the day, break of day, that moment when light overwhelms darkness."

God is telling us that light overwhelms the darkness. Light will overwhelm darkness in your life and the powers of the age to come will be tangibly present in your life because you're walking as a being of that realm.

That light has been introduced to the world and reached maturity in you so the splendor, weight, glory, and honor of the Lord now irradiates you. See and consider the misery, destruction, sorrow, wickedness, ignorance, and death that will cover the earth and the impenetrable gloom of the people. God himself will manifest on you, irradiating and ex-posing His light, His life, His character,

Light will overwhelm darkness in your life and the powers of the age to come will be tangibly present in your life because you're walking as a being of that realm.

His splendor, His weight, His glory, and His honor which will be visible and discerned as inhabiting you. What a promise!

That will draw the masses, the heathen, the nations of the world to be conversant with that brightness and revelation of the Lord that's in and upon you. Kings, royalty, heads of state, leaders of every kind will desire to receive the light of the revelation coming forth from you.

What God is releasing through translocation, translation by faith, and the revelation of your identity in Christ will usher in the final great move of God unlike any revival witnessed. Revival will start in the Church because of the great unbelief in the Church but will turn into a great awakening in the world.

This awakening is for God's purpose, not for the purpose of church growth, kingdom building or making a name for ourselves. The moment it becomes man's purpose, that light switch will be shut off and we'll be living in the natural.

God is releasing a profound insight and revelation, and I'm challenging you by the Spirit of God to grab hold of it! Passionately pursue it, walk in it, and be the forerunner you're called to be. Show the rest of the country what God is doing in the now of your existence, and then show the world!

As people of light, the next time a cyclone is forecast, exercise your authority. You can command it and tell the cyclone, "No! You cannot come this way! Earthquakes, you can't come this way! Drought, you can't come this way!" This is walking in the fullness of who God created us to be.

People asked John Wesley, "How come you're so effective in ministry?"

"Well," he said, "I set myself on fire and stand, and people come to watch me burn." That's what he said!

At the end of the age, this is what we're going to do. We're going to shine like the brightness of the noonday sun, and people are going say, "What in the world is this?" You'll see mass conversions to the Kingdom of heaven and you better be prepared to mentor, steward over, and lead the new believers. This burns in my heart.

We must stop the 10-point program for becoming a Christian: first you accept Jesus, then you get baptized, then you get filled with the Spirit, then you get some gifts. Really? My Bible says when you're born again, it's all done!

Why don't we tell them, "When you accept Jesus with this prayer, you'll be filled with the Holy Ghost, you'll speak in tongues, you'll have the powers of the age to come, you'll have dreams and visions and revelations, you'll be instantly healed and be transformed! And by the way, you should get baptized and follow through with learning Scripture."

If we build the expectation from the front door, instead of walking through the whole house to get to the destination, we'll have a different Church.

A church in Norway is doing this. They say, "Now, when we baptize you, you're going to be filled with the Holy Ghost and you're going to be healed." They come up doing exactly what they've been told. There's a grace for this! We don't need years of discipleship in the movement we have, which is dead works. Ouch!

Let's give them the whole meal deal from the start! That doesn't mean they don't need tutoring and instruction in righteousness. But once you do that, take them along and say, "Now, let's go do these things. You're going to learn and grow."

They're gathering and assembling before you. They're coming to you. Do you see them? There's that word again. Do you see it?

Can you see this by faith? Your sons, your grandsons, your great grandsons—it sounds like longevity to me!

Those you've nourished in the past are coming from remote and distant places. Your daughters, granddaughters, and great granddaughters are returning to receive the impartation of faith and trust. There will be a permanence of the revelatory character they see in you.

Most young sons and daughters are carried so far on their parent's faith, but there comes a crisis moment when they have to make a decision for themselves. Your faith will not carry them into heaven. They must make a choice. Over the years, most of what we modeled for them is rhetoric, but seeing the reality of the Kingdom of heaven will grab them, attract them, and they'll come running back from the place of backsliding because they know it's real.

My wife Reshma was once in Chennai, India with Brother Sadhu Sundar Selvaraj doing a women's conference. When a woman from Malaysia learned that there was going to be a ministry time there, she told her son, "I've got to go! If you're not going to take me, I'm going to go by myself."

The son, an unsaved, rebellious, chain-smoking young man, agreed to take her. He wouldn't come in to the meetings, but sat outside. As the conference continued, some conference workers said, "Brother Sadhu, this woman wants prayer."

"Not now," he said. Reshma, moved with compassion, approached her and prayed for her.

On the last night of the conference, the son was outside talking to some conference attendees. They said, "You know, that smoking will kill you."

Grab hold of God's promises and instruction about translating and walking in the spirit, which is all hinged upon understanding who you are as light.

He scoffed. "I'll quit smoking the day my mother gets healed." He didn't believe any of the faith teachings his mother believed.

After the last song was sung, the meeting was being dismissed when the woman walked up to the platform because God had touched her and healed her. On the large monitors outside the venue, the woman's son saw his mother's miracle on the screen. Weeping, he asked Jesus into his heart. After hearing the Gospel for years, he now saw the reality, which convicted and converted him. Thank You, Jesus!

When miracles and conversions take place, you'll see and be utterly astounded at the overflow of joy that floods your heart, soul, and understanding. You'll be awestricken, as mental restrictions or religious boxes are broken. What a day that's going to be!

The scope of understanding will be enlarged, as the masses and wealth of people will suddenly turn to your favor. Those who have opposed you will support you and the attitudes of those who have doubted you and your integrity in God will utterly change as they're converted to Christ.

The wealth, power, and efficient might of the nations will turn to you as their strength. What an hour to live and what a promise God has given! Grab hold of God's promises and instruction about translating and walking in the spirit, which is all hinged upon understanding who you are as light.

In God's light, there is no time. A brother we know teaches on time and our authority over time. After one woman heard his message, she started experiencing the supernatural. She lived on the East Coast of America and found some shoes that she knew her sister, who lived on the West Cost, would like. After boxing up the shoes, she put them in the mail and drove home.

By the time she arrived home, the phone rang, and her sister said, "Thank you for the shoes! I've been wanting to get those!" Were the shoes translated or did God alter the time? Supernatural events like this are happening around the world.

A couple in England wanted to go on a missions trip and needed their passports by a certain day, which were sent by mail a day earlier. They received their passports in a package, post-marked a week later when they had gone to the post office! "That's impossible!" the postal worker said. "We're very meticulous, and for the government to get anything done that fast is an absolute miracle!" When God says He'll redeem the time, He's going to give you a revelation of light.

—A PRAYER—

BRUCE ALLEN

Because of what God has called me to, I'm going to make a prophetic declaration over you, and it's going to be powerful. I expect testimonies and activations that you'll begin to walk in this. This is my expectation of God. God did not instruct me just to give instruction but to equip and impart what He's given me so that you can walk in these things. As you read this prayer, there's going to be a release of packets of light that will strike and penetrate your spirit, and you're going to take that and begin to walk in this revelation. Though you've been given a lot of information here, know that your spirit has received it.

Father, in the name of Yeshua, right now, under the mantle and authority You have given me, I release to Your people an impartation and activation of this training and this message; that from this moment on, this will begin to explode in their spirits. It will begin to manifest in their lives and will overflow into their families, their churches, their communities, and their nations. Father, release the angelic hosts to bring this promise to pass for the end of the age within their homes. Release them now, Father. I remove scales of unbelief, darkness, and confusion. I remove religious tradition. I remove fear of failure. I remove the fear, doubt, and unbelief that has been the normal portion that we've walked under. No more! Father, they are released to the grace that You have in this hour. I thank You for the springboard that You're placing in front of them that will launch them into the deep. Lord Jesus, I thank You. You're right there with them, fused together with them. They're never alone, and they're not doing this alone, but rather they are covered under the wings of the beloved of the Most High. They're covered as the beloved. Lord Jesus, I thank You for the privilege and the honor of being part of a company of end-time believers that are going to bring powerful and tremendous glory to Your name because we believe. Because we believe. Father, release them in this now. Father, I pray that even today, You will do something supernatural. Translate them. Translocate them. Intervene on their behalf. Thank You, Father. Thank You, Father. And Father, as they gain the revelation of light, I pray the clock would start going backwards in their physical bodies. Show them what it meant when Moses stood in Your presence, that their mortal bodies took on a longevity, strength, health, and vitality. Release this light in them, Father. This revelation is ours. This re-energizing is ours. I thank You for it in the Name of Jesus. Thank You, Father.

The Lord says, "If you can believe, this has been established in you. As you speak forth the mysteries that I have released by faith, you will see an unveiling and an unfolding of the realm of My Spirit that has been yours from the foundation of the world. Now, I release you by promise and decree to walk in it."

Thank you, Father.

—A PRAYER—

RESHMA ALLEN

Father, I pray in Jesus' Name right now. Lord, I come against the spirit of humanism and the reasoning of men. In Jesus' Name. I pray, Father God, also Lord, that You will help us to take away the tastes of the things of this world from our ears, our eyes, and our lives, totally, Father, that we will lose the taste for the things of the world. Father, we thank You for it. We thank You for Your love and sacrifice. Thank You that You have opened our eyes to see, ears to hear, and heart to comprehend in a deeper way. We thank You for the continuation of opening, opening, opening, and taking us to places we've never been before, for entering into the realm of the supernatural. We thank You, Lord. In Jesus' Name, every doubt, fear, and unbelief must go now. No more! It has no place in our lives. No more! We will not give any thought to it anymore. We thank You, Lord. We trust You for everything. We thank You, Lord. We thank You for the release. In Jesus' Name.

ABOUT THE AUTHOR

Dr. Bruce Allen is an internationally known minister of the gospel of Jesus Christ, keynote conference speaker, and best-selling author of several highly acclaimed and anointed books, including the best-seller Gazing into Glory. Dr. Bruce walks in and ministers from the glory realms of God with miracles and signs following. A modern-day Enoch, Dr. Bruce's mandate from the Lord Jesus is to train and equip believers to walk fully in the supernatural things of God, equipping believers to live a life of miracles, signs, and wonders, moving supernaturally across the earth for the purposes and glory of the Lord. Dr. Bruce's passion is to equip and launch believers into their full inheritance in Christ.

Dr. Bruce and Reshma Allen live in Washington, USA and have traveled to over 30 nations of the world, leading those hungry for God into a life of encounters with Jesus Christ and the Kingdom of heaven. Dr. Bruce is the founder of Still Waters International Ministries, has been a guest on, "It's Supernatural," with Sid Roth, and is the host of the popular television program "For His Glory" on Angel TV.

For more information, visit our website
http://stillwatersinternationalmissions.com

OTHER BOOKS BY DR. BRUCE D. ALLEN

Promise of the Third Day

Prophetic Promise of the Seventh Day

Gazing into Glory

Translation by Faith

Foundations of Glory

www.ingramcontent.com/pod-product-compliance
Lightning Source LLC
Chambersburg PA
CBHW070140100426
42743CB00013B/2771